HAUNTED BACHELORS GROVE

HAUNTED BACHELORS GROVE

URSULA BIELSKI

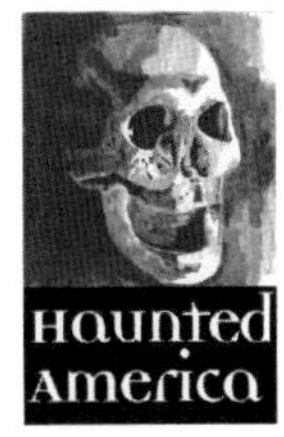

Published by Haunted America
A Division of The History Press
Charleston, SC
www.historypress.net

Copyright © 2016 by Ursula Bielski
All rights reserved

Front cover: Dilapidated but iconic headstone fragments stand sentinel over Bachelors Grove's dead. *Karl K.*
Back cover: The long-gone entrance gate to Bachelors Grove Cemetery, destroyed by 1982. *Photo by Dale Kaczmarek. Insert:* A visitor's token of affection at the Patrick family marker. *Photo by Wendy Moxley Roe.*

Page 10: The front gate to Bachelors Grove Cemetery, circa 1979, three years after the cemetery's condemnation. By 1982, the cemetery sign had been pushed to the ground by vandals. *Dale Kaczmarek.*

First published 2016

Manufactured in the United States

ISBN 978.1.46713.663.1

Library of Congress Control Number: 2016941436

Notice: The information in this book is true and complete to the best of our knowledge. It is offered without guarantee on the part of the author or The History Press. The author and The History Press disclaim all liability in connection with the use of this book.

All rights reserved. No part of this book may be reproduced or transmitted in any form whatsoever without prior written permission from the publisher except in the case of brief quotations embodied in critical articles and reviews.

For Clarence Fulton, who fought for it.
For Matt Allaway, who told me about it.
For Jim Houran. who took me to it.
For Wendy, Karl, Pete, John, Bill and Richie
Who, like me, can't keep it out of their heads.

And…
For Gregory Holmes Singleton
Who taught me that history is what we experience.

In the woods.
It's where you were yesterday, where you will be tomorrow.
The woods is one boundless singularity.
Every bend in the path presents a prospect indistinguishable from every other
Every glimpse into the trees the same tangled mass.
For all you know, your route could describe a very large, pointless circle.
In a way, it would hardly matter.

—Bill Bryson

Watch with glittering eyes the whole world around you
Because the greatest secrets are always hidden in the most unlikely places.

—Roald Dahl

CONTENTS

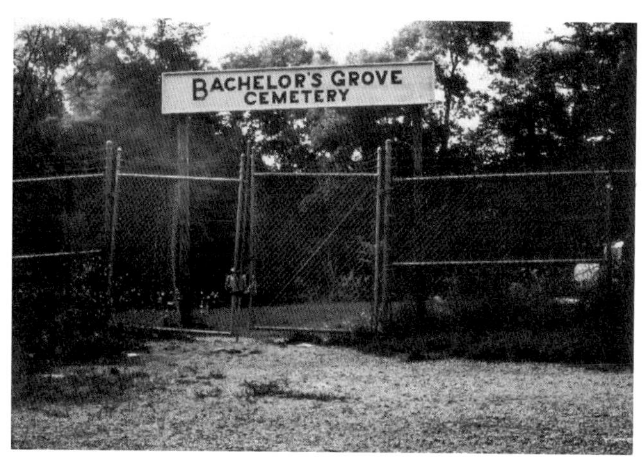
BACHELOR'S GROVE
CEMETERY

PREFACE

Step inside.

In 1996, writing the very first book of Chicago ghost lore, *Chicago Haunts*, I used those words as an invitation, as part of my first chapter. The chapter was about Bachelors Grove, the subject of this book. You could very definitely say that I felt compelled to write that first chapter—that I needed to write it—and that Bachelors Grove, in fact, was responsible for my entire career as a chronicler of the Unknown. This will be important later, as you'll see.

Step inside.

A lot of people remember reading those words when the book was released and, even then, through a page in a book a thousand miles away, feeling the pull of the enigmatic site, through space and through time… pulling, pulling….

I wasn't surprised at this response. I'd felt it, too, many years before, and I still feel it every day—nine books, countless cases and nearly three decades later.

I first visited Bachelors Grove Cemetery in 1988 as a research assistant to parapsychologist Jim Houran (then an undergraduate in psychology), who was performing fieldwork in so-called spontaneous phenomena: the world of experiences including ghosts, hauntings and other anomalous "out of the laboratory" happenings. Over the course of about a decade, we conducted a series of photography experiments at Bachelors Grove, and it was here that I began my proper study of the paranormal and its often complex relationships with human history.

It was a sublime place to start. The isolated, one-acre enclosure had been famous for generations, and with good reason. Since at least the 1960s, whisperings had abounded of what went on at this worn, old ossuary, which lay down a broken path through the woods of a south-side forest preserve, in present-day Bremen Township, southwest of the Chicago city limits. Legends were told of a phantom farmhouse here, seen glimmering through the trees, and of ghost lights flashing blue, yellow and white, which would sometimes chase visitors through the woods. Visitors shared stories of a diaphanous woman in white—the mysterious "Madonna of Bachelors Grove"—who was seen wandering through the woods on moonlit nights, reportedly in search of her baby.

I knew these stories and knew, too, the shadowy half-history of the place. There was the abandonment by its settlers—a first wave of English-born people; a second wave of those of German stock who farmed here well into the twentieth century; the usurpation by the forest preserves; the eventual desecration and destruction; the theft of the crumbling stones; rumors of ritual activity, murder and madness.

As I grew in my studies, history and psychical research meshed ever further, and at some point I became a professional paranormal researcher and historian of the Unknown. The way that I wrote history—interpreted through accounts of the wondrous—gained its own name: "ghost lore."

Twenty-six years after I first visited Bachelors Grove, I've written nine books of ghost lore, founded a company that takes visitors to some of the region's most infamously haunted sites and continue to explore new avenues by which I might teach the dramatic history of ordinary—and extraordinary—people through tales of their brushes with the supernatural.

Along the way, inexplicable things have happened to me, too. Of course, I've seen, heard, felt and even smelled countless phantoms as I've pursued my work, and I've heard thousands of stories of the encounters of others. But it is something deeper than these thrilling (but, in the end, limited) experiences that has proven to me, suddenly and without question, that this is all real.

That something deeper came out of the forest at Bachelors Grove again four years ago, shook me hard and gave me a mission: to find and tell the stories of those buried there, and to find out what secrets the land really held. In essence, to drag the history of the cemetery "out of the woods," where it has been lost for so long.

It was a dangerous quest, at best. Bachelors Grove is known among ghost hunters to have a strange relationship with its fans. Like a best friend, it can welcome one with warm sunshine and camaraderie, as with new friends met on a long Sunday among the broken stones, talking about the supernatural, about the fragments of history to be found there or about nothing at all. It can make you think you've found some sort of home. And then, it can turn on you in an instant, rendering everything as fleeting as mist on the Grove's quarry pond or as twisted as the panels of its chain-link fence.

People change at Bachelors Grove, or perhaps their masks come off there. Whichever it is, the ones close to the Grove know that it is not a place where one should stay long or come often. To do so is to risk losing oneself to its infamous "pull."

In June 2012, after more than two decades of occasionally returning to research Bachelors Grove, I found myself there one muggy night with a steward of the forest preserve, gazing across the quarry pond just before midnight, the unbroken surface lit up only by moonlight. It was perfectly still, and we were totally alone, but I felt the unmistakable presence of others with us. It was one of *those* moments in life, those instants when you feel to your core the great unseen universe just beyond an invisible curtain and realize that, one day, you'll step through and not just feel it but know it, too.

Following a brief stay there, after the moment had left us, we set off again through the woods to our cars. But we became disoriented and, at last, quite lost.

Bachelors Grove is known for disorienting visitors. Even my companion, a steward of the woods for some ten or more years, could not find the way out, though we searched for hours for the trails he himself had marked. We had no light, and even the compass and GPS readings on our mobile phones failed. It was late—or early; the "wee hours" had come. I was wearing a cotton dress, and as we trudged on that hot night, the thorny vines that covered the ground seemed to reach around my ankles, trying to keep me there. It was after some time of this blind searching that we began to see the lights of houses in the distance and to hear the whoosh of cars passing on the road.

Grateful, we routed our path toward the noise, only to have the lights and sounds swallowed up, again and again, as if by a huge vacuum. We were dumbfounded. Somewhere between our cars and this place, we had fallen through an unseen doorway. We were living in a world we couldn't fathom, seeing things that weren't there. The air was close, and time was still going by. But none of it was real.

It was then that we realized we were standing in the heart of Bachelors Grove: a place without direction or landmarks, a place of visions and of memories. It is a place that is sometimes on the map but other times—and quite suddenly—un-findable and un-leave-able.

Bachelors Grove has put me through a lot since I returned there that June night. I've had the most sublime and most harrowing moments of my life in its clutches—and they are clutches; there is no other word for it. I have met both the kindest people I've known as well as the only people I have ever honestly described as "evil": people who turn the truth on its head, without conscience and with impressive will.

It could be said that Bachelors Grove brings out the best and the worst in people. I have heard it said by more than one person—and have come to say myself—that Bachelors Grove eats people.

A lot of people stay away from the Grove because of this strange pull. A few people give in to it, with really bad results.

I do not spend a lot of time in the physical space of Bachelors Grove anymore. For a time, I did. For a time, I felt perhaps more at home there than anywhere else. At some time, however, you realize that you are living in a place meant for the dead.

It begins to show in the living you do.

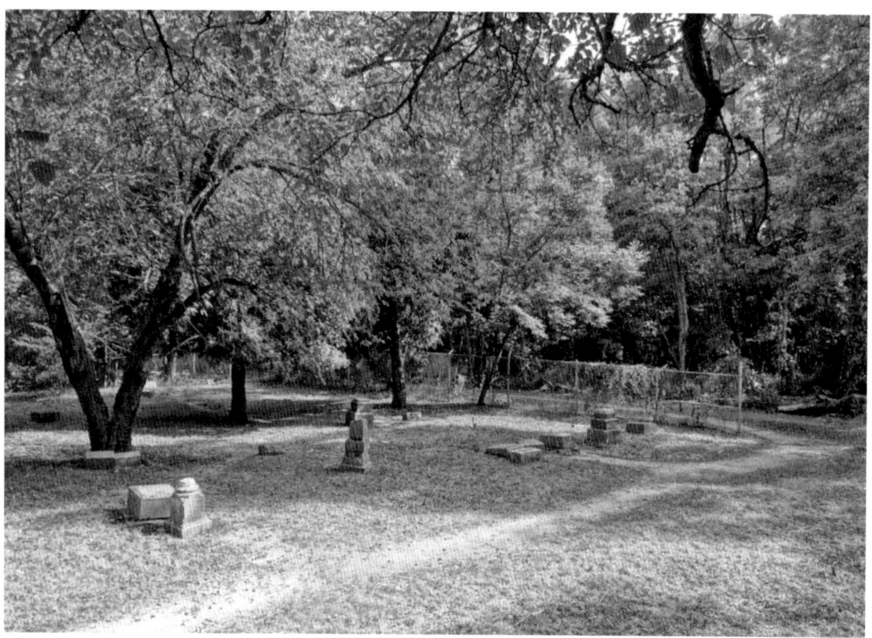

The southeast quadrant of Bachelors Grove Cemetery in 2014, after the county removed most of the plant life in a massive cleanup. Most of the trees, including the famed "split tree" shown here, have now been removed. The two cedar trees seen here (known as "The Pines"), however, still stand as of May 2016. *Karl K.*

Like so many others before me, though, I still wanted to "do" something about Bachelors Grove. Fix it, help it, do something to make things better in some way. But those before me—smarter, more connected, younger, stronger than—had failed to secure the prize we all long for: a restoration, historic designation, honor for the dead and the lives they lived. So, as a practitioner of history who has had bad luck or no luck toward physical change there, I have determined that what I could do would be to take some of Bachelors Grove's negative power away. If I could document the lives of those buried there and bring honor to the dead whose physical space had fallen to desecration; if I could, too, find the real stories behind the looming horror stories that had long been told there, then, maybe, in this way, I could quietly wrest some of the power from the darkness and give it back to those who deserved it: the strong, brave men and women who lived "ordinary" lives of great drama in this enchanted place.

It is my heartfelt hope that, in these pages, you learn something about the people of Bachelors Grove. I hope that, one day, you come to visit them, down that ancient path through the woods, as so many have done through generations. I hope you come away from it all knowing that there is much more to Bachelors Grove than mere ghost stories. And I hope things get better for the place we call "The Grove."

Archaeologist's Note

The Bachelors Grove Landscape: A Path into History

In the northern section of Everden Woods, a nondescript trail leads toward historic Bachelors Grove Cemetery. Situated directly south of 143rd Street, the simple path looks like every other tamed woodland thoroughfare, complete with overgrown side trails extending like river tributaries in every direction, disappearing into thick underbrush. However, unlike most trails within the sixty-nine thousand acres of forest preserves in Cook County, this is an extension of the Midlothian Turnpike. From horse and cart, to motorized vehicles, people traveled this road for 150 years until it was closed off sometime between 1948 and 1950. A new turnpike built just to the north rendered it a simple path leading into the woods.

Today, most people who wander down this path are focused on the cemetery. They are unaware that the physical area around them tells its own story that began long before the cemetery existed. This story does not start with the arrival of European explorers in Illinois in 1673, or even with the influential German, Irish and English settlers of the 1830s. The story rightfully begins with some of the first Illinois residents ten thousand to twelve thousand years ago, on a landscape constantly altered and reshaped by succeeding human and natural forces.

These prehistoric Native American populations were forceful geomorphic agents, heavily impacting the landscape and ecosystem as they developed their settlement and transportation systems in and around what would become Bachelors Grove Cemetery. In essence, the landscape is a human-made artifact, an inherited tradition of culture, collective memories, beliefs and myth carved into the natural environment. It is impossible to precisely know what these memories and beliefs were, because these prehistoric people lacked a written language. However, by interpreting the surviving material culture (artifacts) and natural landscape, it is possible to make educated guesses.

The geographical features of the area were attractive to prehistoric hunting, foraging and farming communities. They settled on high, well-drained landforms in and around the waterways of the Tinley Creek Watershed. These people utilized natural resources such as stone, plants and animals for tools and food sources. The physical evidence of their existence and survival can still be found on the current landscape. To stand in Bachelors Grove and walk the path to the cemetery is to have one foot in the present and the other in the distant past.

For those who visit the cemetery and surrounding forest preserves, please be respectful of the land and the consecrated ground. Illinois law forbids the removal of prehistoric and historic artifacts and the disturbance of human remains, graves and cemeteries on state and federally owned lands. The specific laws are outlined for reference here, via the Illinois Historic Preservation Agency. Here are three extracts from the Illinois Human Skeletal Remains Protection Act:

> *(20 ILCS 3440/4) (from Ch. 127, par. 2664) Sec. 4. It is unlawful for any person, either by himself or through an agent, to knowingly disturb human skeletal remains and grave artifacts in unregistered graves protected by this Act unless such person obtains a permit issued by the Historic Preservation Agency. (Source: P.A. 86-151.)*
>
> *(20 ILCS 3440/5) (from Ch. 127, par. 2665) Sec. 5. It is unlawful for any person, either by himself or through an agent, to knowingly disturb a grave marker protected by this Act unless such person obtains a permit issued by the Historic Preservation Agency. (Source: P.A. 86-151.)*
>
> *(20 ILCS 3440/10) (from Ch. 127, par. 2670) Sec. 10. Any violation of Sections 4, 6 or 7 of this Act is a Class A misdemeanor and the violator shall be subject to imprisonment for not more than 1 year and a fine not in excess of $10,000; any subsequent violation is a Class 4 felony. Each disturbance of an unregistered grave constitutes a separate offense. (Source: P.A. 86-151.)*

Here are two extracts from the Archaeological and Paleontological Resources Protection Act:

(20 ILCS 3435/3) (from Ch. 127, par. 133c3) Sec. 3. (a) It is unlawful for any person, either by himself or through an agent, to explore, excavate or collect any of the archaeological or paleontological resources protected by this Act, unless such person obtains a permit issued by the Historic Preservation Agency. (b) It is unlawful for any person, either by himself or through an agent, to knowingly disturb any archaeological or paleontological resource protected under this Act. (c) It is unlawful for any person, either by himself or through an agent, to offer any object for sale or exchange with the knowledge that it has been previously collected or excavated in violation of this Act. (Source: P.A. 86-459; 86-707.)

(20 ILCS 3435/5) (from Ch. 127, par. 133c5) Sec. 5. Any violation of Section 3 not involving the disturbance of human skeletal remains is a Class A misdemeanor and the violator shall be subject to imprisonment and a fine not in excess of $5,000; any subsequent violation is a Class 4 felony. Any violation of Section 3 involving disturbance of human skeletal remains is a Class 4 felony. Each disturbance of an archaeological site or a paleontological site shall constitute a single offense. Persons convicted of a violation of Section 3 shall also be liable for civil damages to be assessed by the land managing agency and the Historic Preservation Agency. Civil damages may include: (a) forfeiture of any and all equipment used in acquiring the protected material; (b) any and all costs incurred in cleaning, restoring, analyzing, accessioning and curating the recovered materials; (c) any and all costs associated with restoring the land to its original contour; (d) any and all costs associated with recovery of data and analyzing, publishing, accessioning and curating materials when the prohibited activity is so extensive as to preclude the restoration of the archaeological or paleontological site; (e) any and all costs associated with the determination and collection of the civil damages. When civil damages are recovered through the Attorney General, the proceeds shall be deposited into the Historic Sites Fund; when civil damages are recovered through the State's Attorney, the proceeds shall be deposited into the county fund designated by the county board. (Source: P.A. 86-459; 86-707.)

—Dan Melone
Vernon Hills, Illinois

ACKNOWLEDGEMENTS

This book would not have been possible in any way, shape or form without the earlier efforts of Earnest Wilkinson and other students and teachers at Bremen High School in the 1970s. The Bicentennial History Project of 1976, which grew out of their initiative, and their work laid the foundations for all future research, including the extensive mapping of the burials of Bachelors Grove Cemetery by Brad Bettenhausen at the Tinley Park Historical Society, which served as the basis for our own years-long reconstruction of the Bachelors Grove burials included in this book.

Bettenhausen has been the go-to person for information about Bachelors Grove for many years, picking up where cemetery trustee Clarence Fulton and Bremen High School left off, and Bachelors Grove has been fortunate to have such passionate local historians to care about its survival and identity. The Tinley Park Historical Society, staffed by Bettenhausen and a group of dynamic local historians, offered not only wonderful physical resources but also their own extraordinary knowledge. The society remains the number-one resource for information about Bachelors Grove. I have never seen a group of people more devoted to their community's history, and I'm so grateful for both their help with the society's materials and for the many insights they gave into the origins of Bremen Township's oldest settlement area and the lives of its settlers.

The South Suburban Genealogical and Historical Society houses a wide variety of information about Bremen Township. In particular, its large collection of obituaries played a big part in the development of the current burial record contained in this book. Local cemeteries, too, including Zion Lutheran Cemetery in Tinley Park and Mount Greenwood Cemetery in Chicago, were very generous with information and assistance about re-interments and other burial information.

Felicia Ames and her daughter Nicole shared with me the great resources at the Midlothian Library, actually photocopying materials for me and gathering stories from their patrons. For their enthusiastic help, I'm very grateful.

Dan Harper at the University of Illinois at Chicago Archives knows the Forest Preserve District (FPD) Archives inside and out, and it was with his help that I discovered some of the most important documents in the history of Bachelors Grove, including the court transcript regarding the Boehm Quarry. The FPD Archives are a treasure chest of information on Cook County history, and I encourage anyone with an interest in the development of the county to spend some time with the collection.

For tireless effort and the dissemination of so much information to so many, and for providing a place for people to talk about Bachelors Grove, two people have done so much to carry on the interest in and advocacy for Bachelors Grove: Peter Crapia and John Stephenson. Their websites are listed in the bibliography, but if you love Bachelors Grove, you have probably been to them many times already. I have to especially thank Pete, despite all the other unfortunate events that have transpired since then, for taking me to Bachelors Grove to experience one of the most extraordinary few hours in my life. It was that visit that reminded me of how special Bachelors Grove is and that led me to look deeper into its history and mystery.

Many families provided information on the settlement and burials at Bachelors Grove, and without their generous help and their own rigorous research we would not have made the huge progress we have in piecing together the history of the Grove and the cemetery burials. In particular, I would like to thank Bob Schmidt, a descendant of Dorothea and Frederich Schmidt, an avid family historian who well understands that his family is part of a very enigmatic site with a lot of public interest. He so graciously and generously shares his knowledge and family photos with those interested, including for inclusion in this work.

The Forest Preserve District of Cook County and the Real Estate Management Office of Cook County have offered constant support for our events, tours, breakfasts, picnics and cleanups and have issued investigation permits to serious researchers and filmmakers. It is easy to see that they support Bachelors Grove history and research. We are so grateful for their support of our efforts to increase public awareness of this invaluably historic and enigmatic location.

So many institutions supported my research and programs about Bachelors Grove not only by hosting me as a speaker but also by hosting an exhibit of history, artifacts, photographs and more created by Karl K, Wendy Moxley Roe and myself several years ago. I want to especially thank Clay Krueger and Krueger Funeral Home, which hosted the opening of this exhibit and also shared information about and photographs from the final burial at Bachelors Grove in 1989.

It was my dear friend Dan Carroll of the Blue Island Library who first approached Mr. Krueger about hosting the exhibit, and this extraordinary person has truly been one of the most supportive in my entire career. A one-man cheerleading squad, he has celebrated my work at every turn. He and the "Blue Island Gang," as I call them, are some of my favorite people in the whole world, and for their support I'm so grateful. Another incredible person is Vicki at the Ashbary Coffee House in Willow Springs, who opened up her beautiful establishment to us to display our exhibit and talk about the Grove to whoever wanted to come and listen.

Worth Park District History Museum's director, Colleen McElroy, not only hosted my lecture and part of the exhibit but also organized a walking tour of Bachelors Grove for her patrons, which was a joy to host. It is interest like this that keeps me going.

An endless stream of paranormal researchers has found its way to Bachelors Grove, but there are a few very respected individuals who have been examining it for a long time, including Dale Kaczmarek, Chuck Kennedy, Timothy Harte, Mike Hollinshead, Chris Fleming and Jim Gracyzk. I am very grateful for the insights you shared with me. I'd also like to recognize Richard Crowe, of course, who first talked about Bachelors Grove on the radio, during a series of immensely popular radio programs with host Eddie Schwartz. As with so many Chicago stories, it was this series that first brought Bachelors Grove out of being a local, word-of-mouth phenomenon and made it a place of much wider public interest. These interviews provided the first widespread exposure to Bachelors Grove, and he and Eddie Schwartz continue to be Chicago treasures through their legacy and audio imprints.

On this note, I can't really offer enough thanks to local resident Robert Patterson for sharing all of his historic 1970s-era photos and his audio recordings of the Richard Crowe/Eddie Schwartz radio programs. Through these recordings, I was able to pinpoint the origins of several popular Bachelors Grove stories and shed light on some others.

I am eternally indebted to the Wismer family, who offered so much to so many events, including hauling tables, chairs, tents and more down the path in the snow for our wreath-laying event at the Bachelors Grove graves and providing DJ services and equipment, food-service equipment and more for our Bachelors Grove picnic. I call them the "gang of angels," and they truly are.

The professionalism and respect of some of the best researchers has gone a long way in changing the way people view paranormal investigators at Bachelors Grove. They include Paul Mulae, Kenneth Munyer and the Midnight Paranormal Society, who set up nighttime visits through a long process with Cook County; Nicholas Sarlo and Shadow Hunters for their work on the program *True Ghost Stories*; and of course my dear friend Jeff Belanger, *Ghost Adventures'* location scout, who patiently fought through the process to have that wildly popular show visit Bachelors Grove for what would be one of its most-watched episodes of all time.

Linda Romano, who talked with me constantly about Bachelors Grove, shared photos and stories with me, encouraged me at every moment and was always smiling, no matter what. I miss you.

Archaeologist Dan Melone and naturalist Joe Cavataio wrote notes for this book. Every day I'm amazed to have such knowledgeable and generous friends with whom to share my love of Cook County's history, natural or unnatural! Thank you for all you do to enhance both my work and the greater knowledge of Chicago and its surroundings.

Dan, Ron, Colleen, Wally, Ben and Pam, and the rest of the Chicago Center for Psychical Research—my friends and fellow investigators. We need to get the band back together!

I get so excited when I discover something new about Bachelors Grove, such as when I uncover a new family member or a long-lost photo, a portrait of one of the interred or a thread leading somewhere completely different. I want to share it with the world, thinking everyone will be as thrilled as I am. I am so happy to have other people to share this rabid enthusiasm, including Richie (also known as Andy Gump), who calls himself the Ghost of Bachelors Grove. If you have visited Bachelors Grove in the past ten years, you have met him and talked with him. He has picked up thousands of beer and pop cans, cigarette packages and butts, and shared the history of the Grove with hundreds if not thousands of visitors. Thank you.

Thanks to Bill Swinford, who walks the Grove with his beautiful dog, Bailey, each and every day. At all hours of the day and night, I receive text messages from Bill with new information about the Grove, things that recently happened or things he heard. Sometimes he texts me from the Grove and tells me what he's just discovered or what the weather is like. He's like my own personal Bachelors Grove app, with the latest news and info, 24/7. He's also one of the nicest human beings I've ever met, with not a mean bone in his body. His gorgeous wife, Cheri, and their fabulous children are the same way, and they compose one of the best families of all time and the first family of Bachelors Grove today. Thank you for being my friends.

Wendy Moxley Roe and Karl K: we have been together embroiled—no other word—in the drama of Bachelors Grove for almost four years, with some harrowing and some exhilarating moments indeed. We've hated and loved each other, hated and loved the Grove. Sworn it off, got back on the path, kept going, fell off again. Got on again. And here we are. There is only one word for the kind of stuff we have been through together: family. Wendy, your heart is as big as the world, and your keen gift for genealogy—driven by deep love for the people of Bachelors Grove—is a precious gift to the legacy of this magical place. Karl, you only want to make people smile and to bring people together. Bachelors Grove is lucky to have you both to tell its story—and to light it up with your light and love on even the dreariest days.

As in every book, I must thank my daughters, who after so many years have finally stopped rolling their eyes and saying, "Why are you going *there* again?" They now understand that Bachelors Grove is a very special place, and at times I still see a little spark of wonder in their eyes, too, when I talk about Bachelors Grove.

PART I

THE STORY OF BACHELORS GROVE

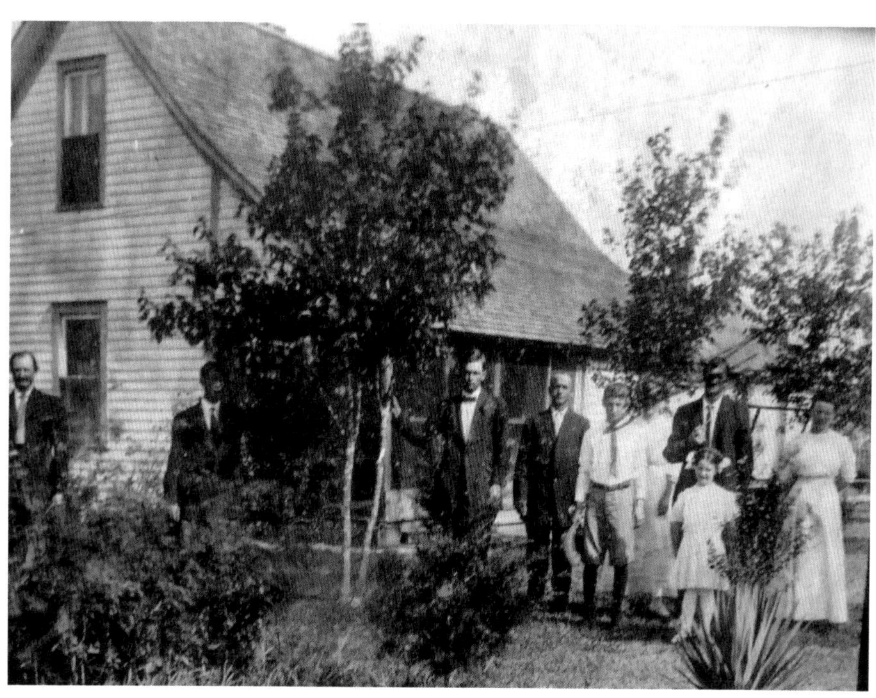

Remains of the homes of the Schmidt family—the last family to own the Bachelors Grove Cemetery land—may still be found off the old turnpike road in a reforested area. The Schmidt family is seen here circa 1915, about a decade before the Forest Preserve District purchased their land. *The Schmidt family.*

1
SETTLEMENT

Cook County, Illinois—which includes the city of Chicago—is home to more than sixty-nine thousand acres of natural and reforested preserve area, the largest forest preserve district in the United States. Hidden in many of these woods of the Forest Preserve District of Cook County are the sometimes plentiful remnants of settlements dating to various periods of history and prehistory, including those left behind during the westward expansion of the nineteenth century. Often, hikers will be surprised by the discovery of house foundations, cisterns and wells, silos and attendant housewares (broken dishes and glassware, furniture, crockery, shingles, tiles and other items) scattered among the flora.

These mysterious reminders of lost lives are truly haunting realities at these hushed enclaves—mute souvenirs of an earlier version of the now-towering city and surroundings. They are almost a funny reminder of the single men and families who were so full of gumption in the most robust period of our heritage; their homesteads today look like trashed hotel rooms, the tenants having gone on to the next party. These were the first settlers of the American West—fearless, bold, far-thinking, at a time when the American "frontier" meant thirty to eighty miles or so west of Chicago. Of all the preserves in Cook County, however, one vanished settlement has always held more than its share of intrigue. Part of today's Tinley Creek Division of the Forest Preserve District of Cook County, the preserve area called Rubio Woods comprises acres and acres of beautiful trails, expansive fields, diverse and beautiful wildlife…and Everden Woods, home of Bachelors Grove Cemetery.

This book is about the one-acre settlers' cemetery called Bachelors Grove and the reforested area of now-public land immediately surrounding it. It's a tiny piece of the world today, but "Bachelors Grove" originally referred to a large parcel of land that included not only the immediate settlement area but also large parts of the area today known as Bremen Township: Tinley Park, Oak Forest, Midlothian, Crestwood and other areas, as well as settlement areas of other townships. Early settlement areas were known by their timber stands—their groves—since harvesting timber was the way the very earliest settlers were able to survive. Farming came later. And so these groves became beacons to prospective settlers, who believed they were made for them, knowing they had a better chance around these natural resources. Part of the original stand of timber at Bachelors Grove is supposed to still exist in Bachelors Grove Woods, a preserve that stands a short walk from the cemetery.

Few of the very first settlers of Bachelors Grove are buried at Bachelors Grove Cemetery; rather, most of that first wave were not really settlers at all, but squatters, who were here a year or two before the first public land sales even happened. Though they did make some of these earliest land purchases, in 1835, most went on to Blue Island, Tinley Park or Joliet or to points farther west: Iowa, Nebraska, even California. These first men and few families came in the early 1830s, mostly through the settlement at Chicago via the Vincennes Trace.

The Vincennes Trace was a major track running through what are now the American states of Kentucky, Indiana and Illinois. Originally formed by millions of migrating bison, the trace crossed the Ohio River near the Falls of the Ohio and continued northwest to the Wabash River, near today's Vincennes, Indiana, before it passed into what became known as Illinois. This buffalo migration route, often twelve to twenty feet wide in places, was well known and used by Native Americans as a major travel route. European traders and American settlers learned of it, and many used it as an early highway to travel into Indiana and Illinois. It is considered the most important of the traces to the Illinois country and, eventually, the larger West.

Myriad impulses drove Americans west in the earliest days: economic hardship in New England and various European points of origin, the desire for land and farming opportunities, overcrowding on the eastern seaboard and, overwhelmingly, the simple desire to move. The tendency of Americans to move, and to move westward in particular, has been studied by some of the greatest social scientists of the last two centuries. But major issues at first held the travelers back: uncertainty about the terrain and prospects was one; the Native American presence was another. While trappers, traders and rogue explorers took on the West in the earliest days—greatly inspired by the expedition of Lewis and Clark under President Thomas Jefferson's administration—most Americans were more timid. The War of 1812 had brought chilling tales of brutal massacres of settlers and soldiers by Native Americans, such as at Fort Dearborn, the future site of Chicago. Many reached the more open lands in Kentucky and Ohio, just beyond the eastern cities, and put down roots there, content with a bit of farmland and a chance to improve their families and futures. Those who ventured farther were rewarded with unrest and, sometimes, terror.

In 1832, the Black Hawk War found most pioneers fleeing to the nearest fort for protection; Fort Dearborn was overrun with refugees, crowded by the dozens into the lakefront cabins of the early traders to await an uncertain future. The Black Hawk War changed a lot for these and other Americans, however, who were chomping at the bit to go *really* west. Shortly after the war ended, a treaty was signed by the Potawatomi, Chippewa and Ottawa tribes, surrendering all territories in northern Illinois and Wisconsin. These huge populations of Native Americans were relocated to acreage west of the Mississippi River after thousands of years of calling these their tribal lands.

With the deals that were made and the relative peace that followed, the western lands beyond the Indian boundary line were now wide open, and there were many, many takers. The years between 1830 and 1850 were ones of massive migration across the United States. The first wave was almost wholly composed of unattached, unhampered single men who went ahead to search for a place where they might have the best chance to make it; families more hesitantly, more sanely, followed later.

For years it was widely held that no settlement or even a single house had existed in the area immediately surrounding Bachelors Grove Cemetery. Visitors wondered at what appeared to be mysterious house foundations in the woods, remains of old wells and silos and fragments of housewares. All sorts of fanciful tales grew out of this apparent disconnect between "history" and evidence. Today a wider population is realizing that Bachelors Grove Cemetery was, in fact, surrounded by a robust community of loggers, farmers and homesteaders who arrived in two waves between the 1830s and 1850s: first, the single men (mostly English and Irish); second, the largely German families who had caught up and, often, moved on to the lands their predecessors had already claimed and improved and then abandoned for points farther west or for larger cities.

Among the many names given the cemetery over the years, "English Bachelors Grove" is an almost forgotten one; yet most of the first property

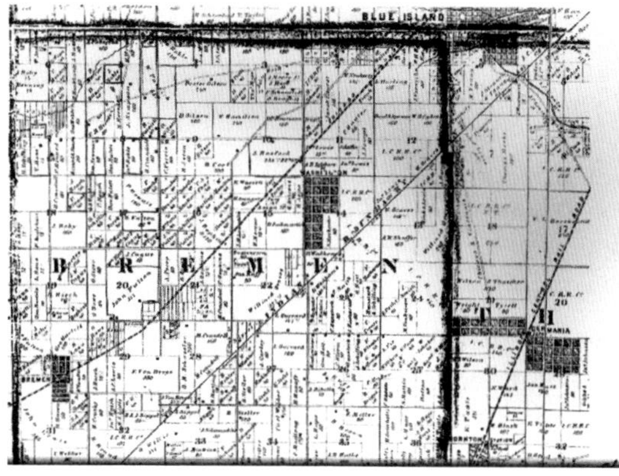

By 1860, Bachelors Grove Cemetery was entering its third decade of service, surrounded by the thriving family farms of Bremen Township, the new name given by the German immigrants who made their homes here during the second wave of settlement, beginning in the late 1830s. *Tinley Park Historical Society.*

holders in Bachelors Grove were, in fact, English bachelors. Despite an enduringly hazy record of the earliest settlers to the area, Stephen Rexford has been commonly considered the first settler of Bremen Township. Rexford arrived at the settlement of Chicago in 1833, two years before the first land sales in Illinois. Like a handful of his like-minded travelers, he chose to go on to the Illinois lands beyond to find his future. He dropped his bag at what is today 159th Street and Cicero Avenue and began to harvest the nearby timber stand: Bachelors Grove. Close behind Stephen was his brother Norman Rexford, who named the future city of Blue Island and built the first substantial structure in town, the tavern that stood on the Vincennes Trace, likely built with timber from his brother's stand.

Brothers Mark, Hemen, David, Alvah and Ethan Crandall walked or canoed from Moira, New York, to Chicago—a distance of some eight hundred miles—in the early 1830s to find land in the Illinois wilds. They were some of a number of young men who went on to the fertile lands outside the bourgeoning city and purchased some of the first land titles at Bachelors Grove in 1835.

McClintock is a name that is familiar to serious researchers of Bachelors Grove because the earliest surviving map of the cemetery was drawn by Eugene McClintock—displayed today at the Tinley Park Historical Society. He and Thomas McClintock are found on lists of the earliest settlers of Bremen Township. The McClintocks, the Crandalls and the Rexfords reportedly planted the first orchard in the area: a grove of peach and other fruit trees recognized by the *United States Agricultural Survey of 1833.*

Other men came after, making the future township of Bremen their destination on the trek westward, and a few made their temporary homes immediately around Stephen Rexford's timber stand. But it was a family

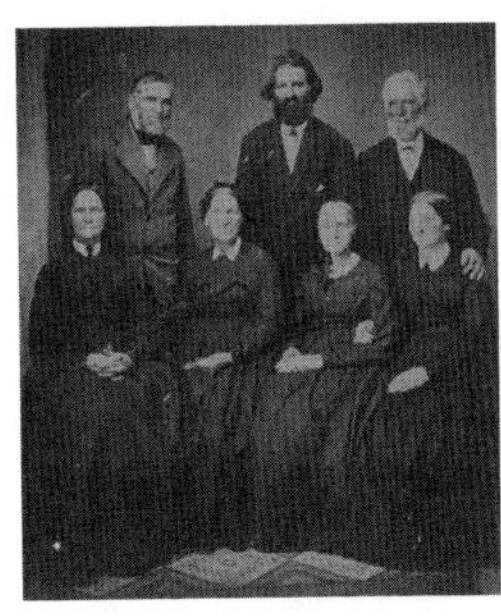

The Crandall brothers—some shown here in a family portrait—walked or canoed from Moira, New York, in the earliest days of Illinois settlement. David and Alvah Crandall advocated for the Bachelors Grove settlers at the first Illinois public land sales in 1835 to ensure that the squatters who had lived on their lands for several years would not be outbid by newcomers. Well known to the settlers at Fort Dearborn (Chicago), numerous Crandall family members were interred at Bachelors Grove but reinterred at Mount Greenwood in Chicago's Beverly Hills neighborhood. Alvah Crandall, however, remains interred at Bachelors Grove. With Stephen Rexford and Dexter Minard, Alvah planted the first orchard at Bachelors Grove in 1833. *Tinley Park Historical Society.*

named Everden who first owned the land on which Bachelors Grove Cemetery was established, as well as the land immediately surrounding it.

The Everdens remain largely mysterious in the annals of Bachelors Grove history. Around 1832, Samuel and Corintha Everden (possibly married or possibly brother and sister) traveled to Illinois from New York with Samuel's two children, Lucinda and Edward Everden, and purchased parts of section 8 in Township 36 during the first land sales of 1830. Their purchases included the cemetery land.

Ironically, it now seems that *Corintha* Everden—a woman—was the first title holder of the Bachelors Grove land. Like Rexford and their other neighbors, the Everdens obtained these lands by patent. This meant that they likely had some connection to the land already when they were offered for the first public sale, just as Stephen Rexford and friends did, having "improved" the land they had squatted on for two to three years before the land sales opened. They were, essentially, getting "first dibs" because they had already been connected to the acreage.

But these first land sales in 1835 were fraught with fear, as there was a question as to whether or not the squatters had perfected their land titles. Though most or all of the squatters had lived on their land for two or more years in most cases and had improved upon the lands—clearing the land for farming, building homes and other structures, etcetera—there were still many vagaries about establishing these definite "ties" to particular land parcels. The settlers at Bachelors Grove and other settlements joined forces before the sale, agreeing that anyone already on a land parcel should be allowed to purchase his land at $1.25 an acre, whether the perfection of the land had been satisfied or not.

The settlers of the frontier appointed David Crandall as their spokesman at the land sale. Crandall was an imposing figure, standing six feet tall in a

207

CERTIFICATE No. 2299

THE UNITED STATES OF AMERICA

To all to whom these Presents shall come, Greeting:

WHEREAS Corintha Everden of Cook County Illinois

has deposited in the GENERAL LAND OFFICE of the United States, a Certificate of the REGISTER OF THE LAND OFFICE at Chicago whereby it appears that full payment has been made by the said Corintha Everden according to the provisions of the Act of Congress of the 24th of April, 1820, entitled "An Act making further provision for the sale of the Public Lands," for the East half of the North West quarter of Section eight, in Township thirty six North, of Range thirteen East, in the District of Lands subject to sale at Chicago, Illinois, containing eighty acres

according to the official plat of the survey of the said Lands, returned to the General Land Office by the SURVEYOR GENERAL, which said tract has been purchased by the said Corintha Everden

NOW KNOW YE, That the **United States of America,** in consideration of the Premises, and in conformity with the several acts of Congress, in such case made and provided, HAVE GIVEN AND GRANTED, and by these presents DO GIVE AND GRANT, unto the said Corintha Everden and to her heirs, the said tract above described: TO HAVE AND TO HOLD the same, together with all the rights, privileges, immunities, and appurtenances of whatsoever nature, thereunto belonging, unto the said Corintha Everden and to her heirs and assigns forever.

In Testimony Whereof, I, Martin Van Buren PRESIDENT OF THE UNITED STATES OF AMERICA, have caused these Letters to be made PATENT, and the SEAL of the GENERAL LAND OFFICE to be hereunto affixed.

GIVEN under my hand at the CITY OF WASHINGTON, the first day of October in the Year of our Lord one thousand eight hundred and thirty nine and of the INDEPENDENCE OF THE UNITED STATES the Sixty Fourth

L.S.

BY THE PRESIDENT: Martin Van Buren

By A. Van Buren Jr. Sec'y.

H. McGarland Recorder of the General Land Office.

The first Illinois land sales of 1835 included land that would be known as Bachelors Grove Cemetery, sold, ironically, to a woman named Corintha Everden. The cemetery was first called Everden's for the owners of the land. When the Everdens sold their land parcels at the Grove in 1864, they did not include the cemetery land in the sale, leading to myriad problems. *Cook County Land Records.*

time when that was giant-like. He was known as a fearless Indian-fighting hulk who once "whipped eleven men by himself and kicked one man clear across the street like a football and killed him." Whether or not this account was exaggerated, we don't know, but we do have a report of what happened when Crandall took a stand at the land sale—and his brother, Alvah, backed him up. An account of it was published in the *Chicago Record* in 1908. It was a very "Chicago"-style event, even then:

> *When the sale commenced the next day,* [an official] *read the terms of the sale. He stood on a balcony, the settlers ranging below. The terms stipulated that any person interfering with or intimidating the highest bidder should be liable to a fine of $500.00 and one year's imprisonment. Excitement was at a fever pitch. The settlers knew some of the land would not stand the legal test, and consequently could be sold to the highest bidder.* [The official] *had no sooner stopped reading when David Crandall mounted a box and cried in a voice out over the prairie, saying, "Settlers, the first man that bids on your land, knock his brains out." David did threaten one speculator by saying, "Just step aside and give me six feet of space. I want to lay out a corpse." The man walked away. Another man did bid $1.30 and Alvah Crandall knocked him down.*

I think it well worth mentioning here that Alvah Crandall is buried at Bachelors Grove Cemetery.

The Everdens got their land, as did all of these other courageous homesteaders in Chicago that day. But the future and fate of the Everdens is largely unknown—as is the origin of the cemetery they left behind. In the 1870 census, I found Samuel, Corintha and Lucinda (or Lurinda) (now thirty-nine) living in Cicero, Illinois, just west of Chicago, six years after the sale of their Bachelors Grove land to Frederick Schmidt. Two children—Albert, thirteen, and Frances, five—lived with them. Their father, Edward Everden, had moved to Chicago to work as a carpenter. I have found no trace of Edward's wife, the children's mother. The family had a rough time of things in general. In addition to his wife's apparent death, Edward's construction company saw tragedy twice. First, his dog bit a little girl on a job site, causing her death from rabies. A second incident involved a construction site accident in which one of his workers was killed. I then found Lucinda as "Lucina" on the 1880 census living in Norwood Township (probably Dunning Asylum), categorized as "insane." That same year, land owned by Lucinda Everden in Bremen Township was put up for sale by the executor of her estate. She must have been committed that year, because earlier that same year she appeared on census records as "single" and still living in Cicero. Albert, twenty-four, was by then married with his own household.

Mark Preston, part of the Bremen High School Bicentennial Project, came to believe that one or more of the Everdens died either on the way to Bachelors Grove or soon after their arrival in 1832, which led to the establishment of the cemetery. It's possible that Everden elders may have traveled with Samuel's family and passed away en route or after arrival or that infant children of Corintha died between 1832 and 1836 and were interred on their land.

No Everden burials are known today at Bachelors Grove; in fact, the whereabouts of the family's remains are a total mystery. For many years, the first known burial was that of Eliza B. Denny, who at sixteen eloped from Kentucky with Leonard Hutton Scott against the wishes of her family. Family lore says they were quickly forgiven and provided with money to purchase land in the wilds of Illinois when they arrived in 1834. Eliza Denny Scott bore seven children but passed away in November 1844, at the age of only twenty-six, leaving behind six little girls. A son, Leonard Jr., also died in 1844, but it is unknown at this time whether Eliza died in childbirth with her son or if the deaths were separate and unrelated. She is buried at the Grove, certainly with her infant child.

They, however, weren't the first. The first known burial at Bachelors Grove was that of William B. Nobles, one of the first settlers of the area. The headstone was stolen or destroyed sometime after 1935; however, he is believed to be interred either in the corner of the southeast quadrant of the cemetery or in the lot of the Cool (Hageman) family, next to the front gate, as his daughter, Jane Nobles Cool, married into their family. Whether Nobles was simply the first casualty of the settlement area or whether he had some connection to the Everdens, we may never know.

What we do know is that his long-gone headstone said he died in 1838. Here we see a typical example of weird Bachelors Grove history. Nobles's obituary—which was published in Schapper's history of Blue Island—clearly said he died on November 9, 1836. This was published over a century ago. Still, for all of the generations that have referenced this note countless times, no one ever really updated this in written histories of the Grove. All of the researchers and historians—including your embarrassed author—who have been "on this case" for so many years never saw that, even though we have all republished this obituary countless times over many decades. No one changed the date of the first burial from 1838 to 1836, until now.

Another nagging question concerns the place-name itself. Generations of historians have sought to uncover the origins of this place's intriguing christening. The cemetery and the settlement have been known by a dizzying array of names: Berzel's Grove and Petzel's Grove; Old Smith's and Old Schmidt's; Old Bachelors and English Bachelors; and Bachelder's, Batchelors, Batchellor's or Bacheldes Grove. It's even been called Crestwood Grove in some genealogical resources. The favorite I've found is "Everdense"—fitting, I think, for such a genealogically confounding site.

Bachelors Grove, however, is the name that has endured, and Stephen Rexford would always claim that the land was named for him and the other single men who settled the area in the early 1830s, traveling first to Fort Dearborn and then on to the prairies beyond.

In fact, other settlements of single men known as "Bachelors Grove" existed in the United States by the nineteenth century, as well as buildings and organizations known as "Bachelors Hall." "To keep bachelor's hall" was an old phrase in common usage by at least the 1790s, when the first known version of the English folk song "Batchelors Hall" (with "t" in the spelling) was composed. To "keep bachelor's hall" meant to maintain the life of a single man, and in various parts of the English-speaking world, the naming of settlements or gatherings of bachelors was already seen by colonial American times. Today, a Bachelors Grove still exists in Grand Forks, North Dakota. Footville, Wisconsin, was originally called Bachelor's Grove (as was its cemetery). An item in the Grand Forks paper in mid-nineteenth-century North Dakota suggested that the name of its Bachelor's Grove was given purposely to try to attract unwed women to meet the lonely single men of the area. The reporter observed that in South Dakota, "marriageable females are as rare as male angels in Washington. There have been several efforts to induce the migration of some of the female surplus in other sections, but the results...have been entirely inadequate."

In a history of Blue Island commemorating the city's first century, John H. Volp writes:

> *Some of the names given to sections of this early settlement were neither as pleasantly descriptive nor, fortunately, as lasting as that of Blue Island. For instance, there were Bachelors' Grove, the "black" or "Robbers Woods" and, worst of all, Horse Thief Hollow. Much to the disgust of the eligible young ladies, many of the young men coming to the settlement in the early days preferred to take up quarters in a section somewhat removed from the Hill, hence the name "Bachelors' Grove."*

Support of the idea that these bachelors deliberately distanced themselves from women had come upon the death of Stephen Rexford's daughter, when the author of her obituary claimed that the men of our Bachelors Grove had actually "taken a vow to remain single"—which most of them abandoned. No other mention of such a vow has been found, however.

What we *do* know is that Bachelors Grove was already known as such when Rexford came, before he even arrived in Chicago in June 1833. That name, though, came at the time with many alternate spellings, suggesting that the place may have been christened with a surname and not named for a gathering of single men. At the Methodist conference held in Jacksonville, Illinois, in 1832, a Reverend Stephen Beggs of Walker's Grove was put in charge of the Des Plaines Mission—for the area around the Des Plaines River, presumably, which included a place called "Batchelor Grove." An 1834 *Gazetteer of Illinois* reported that "Bachelder's Grove, in Cook County, eighteen miles southwest of Chicago, contains about two sections of timber and a large settlement," demonstrating yet another variation of the name attached to the Grove—and supporting the idea that the Grove was named for a person and not for a single man or group of them. It must be noted that by the spring of 1833, Stephen Rexford, Thomas McClintock, Alvah Crandall and Samuel Everden were recorded by the *United States Agricultural Survey* as having planted a grove of peach and other fruit trees at "Batchellor's Grove" (mysterious, since Rexford did not arrive until that summer). Again, this spelling suggests a surname rather than a gathering of bachelors.

But if this was the case, who was this mysterious "Batchelor," "Batchellor" or "Batchelder," and where did he go? No Batchelders or Bachelors or Batchelors show up on the earliest property or settlement records of the area. Some Batchelors and Batchelders from New England did settle in Illinois, but in LaSalle County, Macon County and Winnebago Country. Batchelders found in Cook County's Rich Township in the latter half of the century were from another, later migration line. Some Batchelders and Foots who came to the Illinois lands went on to found Batchelors Grove (today called Footville) over the Wisconsin border—which also had a Bachelors Grove Cemetery, now Footville Cemetery. Other Bachelors went famously to the Dakotas, where that Bachelors Grove still exists today in Grand Forks, where those unfortunate men couldn't catch a break.

I thought I'd hit pay dirt when I found a man named Edward Batchelder, a Vermont teenager who went to Boston to apprentice to a jeweler but ended up going on "to the wilds of Illinois" with his wife and infant daughter. He settled about thirty miles south of Chicago in Thorn Grove, an area about ten miles from Bachelors Grove Cemetery. Working off a timber stand, the family only stayed four years before going to Chicago to live. Batchelder lost everything, including his home, wife and three of his four children, in the Great Fire of 1871. Born in 1811, I figured that, if he left Boston at eighteen and stayed in Thorn Grove for four years, this would have put him in the Bachelors Grove area in 1828 or 1829 and leaving for Chicago by 1832. Batchelder would have moved into Chicago by the time Stephen Rexford arrived at Fort Dearborn. They likely would have met in one of the taverns of the day. Surely this had to be the Batchelder I'd been looking for. Alas, upon further research I discovered that Batchelder hadn't left New England until after 1835, at least two years after Rexford had already gotten to Bachelors Grove, and more than three years after the famed Reverend Beggs was sent to the Illinois settlement of "Batchelors Grove" as a missionary.

But it is Beggs who takes us down another road to look for our mysterious namesake.

Other timber stands, both in Illinois and around the nation, bore the names of preachers of the time, such as Walker's Grove, present-day Plainfield, a bit farther south of Bachelors Grove. Reverend Jesse Walker, "The Daniel Boone of Methodism," was a circuit rider who traveled throughout Missouri and Illinois on horseback, spreading the gospel message. As a missionary to the Indians, Reverend Walker followed the Illinois River on horseback. In 1829, his son James Walker and ten settlers formed the first Methodist class in "Walker's Grove," now Plainfield.

Beggs, who was sent to convert the Indians and settlers at Bachelors Grove in 1832 and ended up in a battle of the Black Hawk War, was an associate of one of the more active preachers of the early northwest wilderness, a man named Wesley Batchelor. Batchelor went on to be the first pastor of the church at Ottawa, in LaSalle County. These two men, along with numerous other preachers, would have been well known and well traveled between Chicago and LaSalle County. But was Batchelor already working in 1830 or 1831, before Beggs was sent to the settlement that bore the Batchelor name? Quite possibly, as he was listed as one of the "superannuated or worn out preachers" in the minutes of the meetings of the Methodist Conference of 1852–55.

Whatever the origins of Bachelors Grove's name, the settlement did not remain remote for long. In the years that followed the first arrivals, thousands of settlers poured into the area. It is obvious that most of these settlers were German immigrant farmers, who of course soon affixed to the place a name from their beloved homeland: *Bremen*. They had been farmers by trade in

Germany; with farmland scarce in their homeland, the fertile open lands of the United States were impossible to resist. A.T. Andreas wrote about it in his 1884 *History of Cook County:*

> *Bremen comprises within its limits a fine agricultural district, being situated in the most fertile portion of the county. It has a finely diversified surface, swelling prairie alternated with groves of timber instead of the level plain, which is often characteristic of the prairie portions of the State.*

The English and Irish settlers remained a big part of the settlement, too, though most went on to live in the cities of Blue Island and Tinley Park or went on to points farther west. A plat map of 1861 Bremen township shows the incredible settlement that had followed the first land sales of 1835. Among the family and individual names of the early settlement are many of the dead of Bachelors Grove Cemetery: Fullerton, Rippet, Cool and others. Also found here are the homesteads of the Fulton family, arguably the most prominent of the early area settlers, a number of whom are buried at Bachelors Grove. Here, too, is the homestead of the Funk family; undertakers by trade, they prepared many of the Bachelors Grove burials from the Funk Funeral Home in Tinley Park. Their own burial ground may still be seen in town, behind a housing subdivision. One of the two crucial families in the history of Bachelors Grove Cemetery was the Schmidt family, who purchased the Everden land, minus the acre housing the cemetery. The remains of the Schmidt homestead may still be found along the path to the cemetery. Death and burial records from the late nineteenth and early twentieth centuries often name the burial site of Bachelors Grove as "Schmidt's Cemetery" or "Old Smith's," as it was sometimes known by local residents.

Until the eventual burgeoning of New Bremen (Tinley Park), the center of the farming community of Bachelors Grove was Goeselville, where a German immigrant named Christian Goesel built a general store in 1868, near the intersection of 147th Street and Ridgeland Avenue—the edge of the cemetery forest boundary. The tiny spot—its largest population was about thirty people—boasted its own post office, and it sold everything, even headstones, from its shop, which catered to local farmers. Like the rest of Bachelors Grove, Goeselville was short-lived, eventually absorbed by Oak Forest and the Forest Preserve District of Cook County. By the time of the Civil War, the railroads had enabled travel between Chicago and Joliet, and the prevalence and importance of Bachelors Grove was no more.

Most of the holders of the first land titles had moved to the larger towns of New Bremen, Blue Island or points farther south. Some had gone back to Chicago to seek their fortunes in the now-bustling metropolis. Some had gone to Iowa, Nebraska or even California. Bachelors Grove, by the close of the nineteenth century, was already largely a has-been: a proud and crucial early outpost now prone to whatever history had in store.

For many families and individuals in the former "wilds of Illinois," that meant continued, gradual abandonment by homesteaders and eventual submission to one of the most mammoth and complicated projects in Illinois history: the planning of the Forest Preserve District of Cook County.

2
REMOVAL

The development of the largest forest preserve area in the United States came at a massive price for many private landowners of Cook County, Illinois, who, despite the ongoing exodus of neighbors, did not want to leave their lands, their homes or their heritage. Though some families went easily, charmed by the large sums exchanged for extensive acreages, the Forest Preserve District (FPD) of Cook County archives are full of legal files covering the painful removal of longtime settlers and homeowners from their property via eminent domain and the condemnation and seizure of their land and homes.

The cemeteries of Cook County that had been swept up in the forest preserve land sales, including Bachelors Grove, were of precious little more concern than the properties of individual citizens and families. Indeed, the language used in early dialogue about the subject is rather appalling to our sensibilities today. But to understand why Bachelors Grove's fate happened, it's necessary to see that the whole plan for these cemeteries was for them to eventually disappear.

In August 1925, Ramsone Kennicott, an official of the Forest Preserve District of Cook County, spoke to a meeting of the Association of American Cemetery Superintendents, clearly expressing the plan for the cemeteries the district had acquired through condemnation:

> *We have the right of eminent domain and it doesn't make any difference how much some farmer wants to hold his farm or how much some private*

> *citizen wants to hold his house, if it is considered best for the greatest number of people, we go ahead and condemn the land and take it, and the only thing that does stop us are the cemeteries. We find that they make a dead line. That doesn't bother me, personally, so much, because with all due respect to our dead, with all due respect to this group of people who are interested in that particular thing, I believe that one hundred years from now our cemeteries in Cook County will all be parks, anyway. I would be very glad to know that a lot of Boy Scouts would tramp over my grave, and I think that one hundred years from now maybe our ideas of cemeteries will change and that we will all be glad to have them used as parks.*

Not all settlers were against the FPD plans. Bob Schmidt, a descendant of Frederich and Margaretha Schmidt, confirms that his family had little problem with vacating the land they had purchased from Everden in 1864. For the exchange, the family received in excess of $125,000 (about $1.7 million today). But there were two big issues with this land sale, because it concerned two other entities over which the Schmidts had no control. One of these entities was the cemetery itself, which was not part of the Forest Preserve District sale. And there now seems to be more to that story than we thought.

In light of recent research, it seems entirely possible that there were burials at present-day Bachelors Grove Cemetery *before* the Everdens purchased the land from the government in 1835 and that even the Everdens themselves may not have considered the burial area as part of their land to begin with. In the 1970s, elderly residents went on record claiming to have seen at least one grave marker at Bachelors Grove with a death date of 1832, possibly more. One of the Fulton family members asserted that many of the Grove's stones were not erected until years after the deaths occurred, and Bachelors Grove researcher Wendy Moxley Roe pointed out an important fact: many early cemeteries utilized wooden markers, saplings or stones to mark graves unless the interred were very wealthy. It is highly probable that at least some such markers were used here but were irreparably damaged over time, eventually disappearing entirely. These markers may even have been gone by 1864, when the Everdens sold the surrounding land to the Schmidts and the first plat map of the cemetery was drawn.

Even more intriguing is that at least two sources have claimed that Bachelors Grove Cemetery was a Native American burial ground before it was used by European Americans. Early maps of Cook County do not show Indian mounds here (though they do exist in Rubio Woods slightly

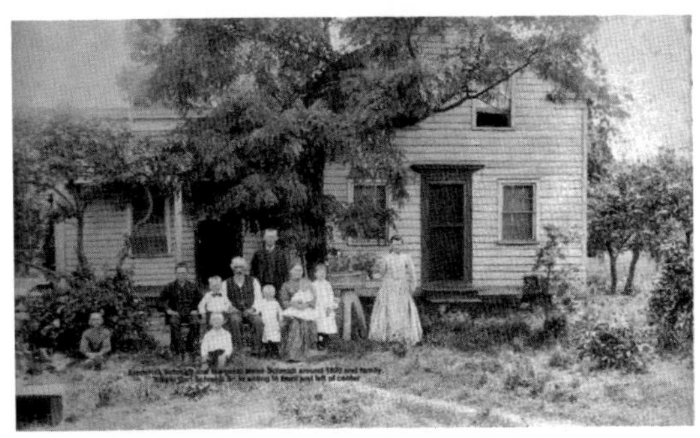

Frederich and Margaretha Schmidt, shown here with their children in the 1890s at their home in Bachelors Grove, purchased the Everden land in 1864. After the sale, a first plat of the cemetery was drawn by Eugene McClintock, but it is uncertain whether the land was ever dedicated as such. When the Schmidts sold their land to the forest preserve decades later, they followed the lead of the Everdens and did not include the cemetery in the sale. *The Schmidt family.*

north), but as archaeologists point out, maps are of little use in determining Native American land use, since most only date to the late eighteenth or early nineteenth century, while Native American peoples were present for thousands of years. In 2014, local resident Bill Swinford met a young Native American man in the woods west of the cemetery who said he was camping in the area for a few days. Swinford warned the young man that he would be fined or even arrested if found camping on Forest Preserve District property. The young man told him this was of no concern to him, that this was his ancestors' land and that others were the trespassers. On another occasion, Swinford met a young Native American couple, dressed in business attire, who walked across the creek and into the woods. After being gone for about thirty minutes, the couple retuned with animal bones in a bag. Curious, Swinford mentioned that he had found a deer bone earlier that week, after which the couple talked about the energy contained in bones, though they shared nothing about why they had removed their own specimens. Could these curious visits indicate a much older tribal site?

The other issue with the Schmidt sale was also contained in the warranty deed. Besides the cemetery land, the deed also excepted a small parcel of land that had been deeded to a man named Frederick Boehm in 1909. After exhausting every possible research avenue over many years to determine the nature of this exception, I discovered in the archives of the FPD legal files a 115-page court transcript from 1928 that, amazingly, specifically dealt with this very acreage. As it turns out, this was the land that contained the present-day quarry "pond" at Bachelors Grove: a murky, water-filled "hole in the ground," as one witness scoffed during the hearing. Frederick Boehm, a local farmer, had died in 1925, presumably leaving the land to his son Christian (or Christ) Boehm. Other Boehms lived mostly in nearby Worth village, as well as in Chicago, where Christ's brother George ran a grocery store and where Frederick lived at the time of his death. According to the testimony, Christ had created the quarry around 1909 and had operated it on and off until the early or mid-1920s, then moving to Knox, Indiana, to work as a builder. According to neighbors, by 1928 the quarry had been closed for several years, its rusting equipment abandoned. Boehm had been sent the usual offer letter from the Forest Preserve District: Go quietly or have your property condemned. To which Boehm responded with a handwritten note expressing shock at the lowball offer: "There must be some mistake."

Boehm informed the county that his land included a stone quarry that he'd created himself and that these land sales were to include such improvements to the land, as well as houses and other buildings, farms and gardens and anything they contained. Many sellers—some opportunistic, some just really angry—tacked on lists of such, which included everything from "seven rose bushes" to "three coats of premium pant on the parlor wall." Some lists literally included the kitchen sink. Many sellers, too, insisted on money to move their houses. During my years of research on Bachelors Grove, I have sometimes run into people who have claimed their family homes once stood in Bachelors Grove but had been moved into town—to Crestwood or Midlothian or Blue Island. I found this inexplicable and strange until reading the many files of correspondence and conflict over the forest preserve deeds.

Boehm won. For his land and his house, and for his enigmatic "hole in the ground," he received $2,000 per acre and $5,000 for improvements: a total of $15,000, two and a half times the county's original offer. After the determination, he left Cook County and never looked back.

3

Obscurity and Celebrity

In my reading of the court transcript discussing the Boehm Quarry at Bachelors Grove, one thing became very clear: by the time the Forest Preserve District sent its condemnation letters, there were very few people actually living at Bachelors Grove. In fact, Christ Boehm didn't even know the names of his own tenants, while neighbors expressed no more than a passing knowledge of the area's inhabitants. They couldn't even remember how long the quarry had been inoperative.

This once-thriving community of close-knit settlers had dramatically transformed, and like most everything else in that era, the change was tied directly to the railroads. For while it has long been presumed that the closing of the old Midlothian Turnpike was the cause of what would become a seemingly endless era of desecration and unrest at Bachelors Grove Cemetery, the trouble actually began long before the closing of the road. To understand it all, we must start at the Midlothian Country Club, for which the road was named, and which would be one of the most influential developments in the history of Bremen Township.

At the Chicago World's Fair of 1893, Americans first encountered many cultural curiosities. The game of golf was one of them. Enraptured, businessmen—and well-heeled women—established a quick and impressive following for this "new" pastime. In 1889, Harlow Niles Higinbotham—the president of the World's Columbian Exposition, director of the Northern Trust Bank and partner at Marshall Field & Company—proposed the creation of a golf club to be built outside Chicago. A landscape architect was chosen, and a site was earmarked, less than a mile from Bachelors Grove Cemetery. Some histories suggest that the site was specifically chosen for its remoteness, that the directors did not want the usual country club set to know about the development. But the Midlothian Country Club quickly became a sensation, not only in Chicago but around the world.

Immediately, the problem of actually *getting* to the club became a big one. Before the building of the Midlothian/Blue Island spur line (MBI Railroad) to bring country club guests to the grounds, visitors had to take the train to Rexford's Crossing and travel the last leg over dirt roads. Those coming from Blue Island took the Midlothian Turnpike, an ancient Indian road called the "Old Blue Island Road" on the first maps of Cook County. This road led from Blue Island, diagonally southwest through Bachelors Grove (and past the cemetery). Many made use of the club's famed "Tally Ho Wagon," a rather ramshackle-looking vehicle that required as many as six horses to pull it through the often muddy trail. After the building of the rail extension to the country club, the turnpike was used less and less, and almost exclusively by travelers on foot going to Blue Island to catch the train to Chicago to work or shop. In 1927, 147th Street was paved, creating the first paved street in the area and making both the spur line and the old roads obsolete. This same year saw the closing of most of the sales of private land to the Forest Preserve District of Cook County and the final vacating of most of the area homesteads.

It wasn't until 1941, however, that the FPD revealed plans for the future of the district; maps from that year clearly show the turnpike road "to be abandoned." But some evidence suggests that, by that time, there may have already been trouble—and ghost stories—brewing on this once busy highway.

According to an *Examiner* article published in October 2012, a man named Huburt Geist claimed to have started the haunting tales of Bachelors Grove as far back as the 1930s. According to the author of the article, Geist had written a pamphlet in that era and distributed it to area libraries. In his pamphlet, Geist said that he'd come to the area in the 1870s and opened a blacksmith shop, tending to horses traveling the old turnpike road between Blue Island and the pioneer settlements. With the coming of the country club and the motor age, he opened a filling station and continued his roadside service. However, when the road fell into disuse after the building of the rail line, he found that, often, the only travelers on the road were young people, high on bootleg gin, most of them the kids of the country club set who would drive to Bachelors

Grove Cemetery from 147th Street and park, engaging in all sorts of untoward behaviors, most of which Geist claimed he could overhear. He decided to take matters into his own hands. One night, he crept through the woods with a lantern, making "hooing and booing" sounds, thoroughly scaring off a young couple in the throes of mischief. Greatly satisfied, Geist made this a nightly ritual—until it backfired on him. To his chagrin, young people began coming to the area purposely to "look for spooks," and the more he tried to scare them off, the more they came. Moreover, the new crowd didn't seem to be afraid of spooks at all: the first wave of Bachelors Grove's ghost hunters, it seems.

Backing up these stories, researcher Wendy Moxley Roe interviewed one elderly gentleman in recent years who shared that, by the late 1930s or early 1940s, it was common practice to meet young women at the Bachelors Grove dance hall and picnic area—where Carlson Springs Preserve is today—and then walk the girls to the cemetery to scare them. The popular spot (which featured barbecues, "beer by the pitcher" and Hawaiian and country-and-western musical acts) was at the edge of the forest preserve land, and these young people would have walked along the old turnpike road and over the creek bridge to reach the cemetery. In light of these circumstances, it now seems likely that by the time the Midlothian Turnpike was scheduled for closure, there had already been revelers and even ghost hunters coming to the cemetery at night for a number of years, using the turnpike road and the bridge over the creek.

In addition to the moral issue of young people visiting the cemetery at night, there was something else that was happening at the cemetery in this period that likely made the issue of the cemetery a troubling one. A 1935 local newspaper article, entitled "Pioneers in Peaceful Rest," provides the clue. In the article—a sort of armchair tour of the cemetery—the reporter writes that the Patrick family stone was already "broken off." That same article describes the cemetery as quiet but not very well preserved, suggesting that many of the stones were already showing signs of damage. Whether this damage came from age or human hands, we don't know, but the article does demonstrate that in 1935, the physical condition of the cemetery was more of an issue than were any teenaged shenanigans. Indeed, the subtitle describes the cemetery as "serene" and "undisturbed," though we know that Bachelors Grove Cemetery had a popular following by then as a point of interest for local young people.

Part of the heightened interest in Bachelors Grove Cemetery was also surely due to the exposure it had received in April 1934, when readers

BACHELOR GROVE

Presents

Another OKEDOKE PARTY

Next Monday Night, August 11

STARS Galore—from a number of Radio Stations — and all the Old-Timers will be there.

SPECIAL MUSIC • ENTERTAINMENT

BEER BY THE PITCHER

No Cover or Min. Earl Leider, Owner

145th and Oak Park Ave.

West of Blue Island on 147th St.

Young people began visiting Bachelors Grove Cemetery at night in the 1930s, driving out in the evening from the Midlothian Country Club nearby. By 1940, the cemetery was already known to local young people as "haunted," drawing revelers from the popular Bachelors Grove dance hall and picnic grove, located in present-day Carlson Springs Preserve. The young people would walk through the woods and over the creek to "look for spooks." Southtown Star.

around the nation first heard of this tiny burial ground via none other than the great Robert Ripley. The cemetery appeared in Ripley's illustrated column, Believe It or Not!, as the article marveled that "women are buried in the Bachelors Grove Cemetery, Midlothian Turnpike, Illinois." Ripley had gained a whole new audience in 1933 when he unveiled his first "Odditorium" at Chicago's Century of Progress World's Fair: a collection of curious artifacts gathered from cultures around the world. (One wonders if Ripley, who had many well-heeled Chicago friends, may have traveled to the Midlothian Country Club and heard about the cemetery—or even visited it—himself.) At the time, the appearance of a local site in an international news publication—the enormously popular Ripley's column, no less—would have been an exciting event indeed, especially for the numerous locals who had explored his Odditorium at the World's Fair. In fact, the local Tinley Park paper featured a brief column *about* the column, also referring to the cemetery as "Smith cemetery."

In these sensational times we also find the first rumors of another type of visitor to Bachelors Grove: gangsters from Chicago who reportedly dumped bodies from the quarry overlook at Bachelors Grove, a legend that persists into the twenty-first century. Though no news reports have been found to substantiate this specific claim, the extreme violence of the gangland era was brutally evident in Bremen Township. Local papers were filled with the reports common to almost every town in America: the tales of tragedy peppering the Prohibition era. Each week, stories appeared of the explosion of homemade stills or "cookers," raids on their operators and bullet-riddled bodies of rivals found dumped along the desolate roads of Tinley Park, Oak Forest and Orland Park. The Tinley Park Historical Society clippings files contain some of these articles from unknown local publications. On October 21, 1927, a local paper reported that Fred Passini—an alcohol "cooker" or bootlegger—and a companion were found murdered fifteen hours apart. Passini had been "taken for a ride" and his body pitched into a ditch at 167th Street and Cicero Avenue, just ten blocks from Bachelors Grove. He had been shot in the head nine times. His companion had been found at home, shot sixty-nine times with a shotgun. The next summer, police reported on the latest victim of the "savage feud that has marked the struggle for control of the liquor traffic in the territory." An unidentified man had been found by a farmer and his son near 179th Street and Central Avenue. He had been tossed from a car, as evidenced by the broken bushes under him, and more than a dozen machine-gun bullets were lodged in his skull and shoulders. We know from other researchers that at least one local resident, a dairy owner, moved out of the area because of threats from Al Capone's rumrunners, who ran a "milk route" as a cover for liquor delivery and didn't want any competition.

From homestead sales and settlement shifts to the building of roads and railroads; from reforestation and isolation to national celebrity and gangland intrigue—we can probably never know the complex details of what led to the downfall of Bachelors Grove Cemetery. But I feel one can only conclude this: while the disappearance of settlers and the decrease in traffic along the turnpike road after 1927 did lead to its isolation and popularity as a lovers' lane and gathering spot, the actual closure of the turnpike road from 143rd Street to Ridgeland Avenue after 1941 happened in tandem with existing decay and notoriety at Bachelors Grove Cemetery. It was not the initial cause of it, as has long been claimed. In fact, it may even be that these very issues—nighttime visitors, national renown and the precarious state of the cemetery—contributed to local and county desires to close the road. But that closure just made everything worse.

4
DESECRATION

On September 11, 1952, the first known newspaper article announcing vandalism at Bachelors Grove Cemetery appeared in the *Blue Island Sun Standard*. However, the article clearly stated that vandalism had been going on for several years at the time of the report and that it was enough of an issue by 1952 that law enforcement was making daily visits to curtail visitors:

> *Vandals knocked down at least 10 granite monument headstones in old, historic Bachelor's Grove cemetery on 143rd st. in Bremen Township, sometime last week. The desecration was discovered when cemetery officials went to repair a fence Friday evening, that had been reported damaged. Several headstones were knocked* [sic] *weighed at least 800 pounds. Many old Blue Island families are buried in this ground.... One of these was knocked over several years ago and set up again after much labor and expense. One of these was knocked over a second time. Police are attempting to check the cemetery nightly to keep out intruders.*

On April 3, 1958, the *Sun Standard* reported that several of the stones had been broken off and other smaller headstones pulled out of the ground and scattered around the confines of the cemetery. In 1965, the *Chicago Tribune* reported:

Vandals Damage

Bachelor's Grove Cemetery

Extensive damage to many markers and monuments in the more than a century old Bachelors Grove cemetery at Midlothian Turnpike and 143rd st. has been noted by the trustees.

Some of the smaller markers have been pulled up and scattered. Some of the larger old pieces have been chipped off and deliberately broken.

The vandalism occurred only recently. Arthur A. Fulton, 4445 W. 142nd st., a trustee, said that the trustees would try to arrange for the picking up of the scattered headstones as well as they can.

Much of the damage is irreparable.

Many Blue Islanders have relatives buried there.

The cemetery is still in active use. There is at least 200 graves there, some of them a century or more old.

The first published report of vandalism at Bachelors Grove appeared in the 1950s, but cemetery trustees had by then been waging a private war against it for years. *Chicago Tribune.*

> *Homewood sheriff's police began an investigation yesterday of desecration of graves in Bachelors Grove Cemetery, just south of 143rd St. near Midlothian Turnpike in Bremen Township. Sheriff deputy Howard Vanek discovered that a fire had been built in the cemetery early yesterday. A coffin handle and hinge were found in the ash. Nearby, in freshly turned soil, a coffin was found about 4 inches below the surface. Witnesses told police youths were digging in the cemetery late Saturday and early Sunday.*

By September 14, 1973, the digging up of graves was yet continuing, with the *Tribune* reporting:

> *Sheriff's police seized seven teen-agers Wednesday night in Bachelor Grove Cemetery, 143rd street and Ridgeland Avenue. The police said the youths were there to complete digging up a grave. Sgt. Lawerence Evans and Juvenile Officer James Houlihan staked out the gravesite after a squad car on patrol late Tuesday night noticed that about five feet of earth had been removed from the grave. The policeman said the youths arrived Wednesday night, got out, and prepared to resume digging when the policemen announced themselves. The youths told police they were doing it "as a lark." The two young men, of Burbank, were charged with destroying a tomb. They were released on $1000 bonds.*

Year after year, report after report appeared in both the local papers and the *Chicago Tribune* and other major papers, alongside the shocking photos of the dirty work of vandals: desecrated stones, unearthed graves, fire pits filled with the debris of drinking parties—and the first publicized ghost stories of what would become known as one of the "world's most haunted places." Though ghost stories had lived at the Grove via oral reports for perhaps as long as two decades by the time of the first publicized desecration, it is uncertain if the destruction or the stories started first, but it seems likely that several factors converged to set off the era of decline.

First of all, the cemetery—which had been along a well-traveled public way since its inception—was now at the dead end of a crumbling road. Though I have not been able to find in the forest preserve records any administrative orders to remove the turnpike bridge and close the road, these events were set in motion sometime between 1941 and 1951. Drawings from the former year exist in the FPD records designating "road to be abandoned" from 143rd Street to Ridgeland Avenue. And in 1951, a deadly accident occurred when a car full of travelers mistakenly took the turnpike road across the creek, not realizing the bridge had been removed. Also by 1951, the cemetery would have been largely hidden from outside view by re-forestation, providing increased cover for deviant activities.

It was not until the early 1960s that the Midlothian Turnpike was reconfigured to feed into 143rd Street, bypassing the forest and the cemetery, though vehicle access to the cemetery over the old dirt road was still possible until 1977. It was after the 1960s reconfiguration that the worst vandalism and desecration began, which is likely why historians have long credited the "closing of the Turnpike" for the downfall of the cemetery, though this was one of the later stages in a closure that happened in stages over many years, in tandem with re-forestation and its own isolating effects.

5

The Struggle for Bachelors Grove

The precarious situation of Bachelors Grove Cemetery had not escaped local notice. As we've seen, damage to various stones was already noted by 1935, and by the late 1940s, vandalism had been confirmed. By the early 1950s, destructive activity at the cemetery was an issue of serious concern to the cemetery's "trustees." According to local reports, a private board of trustees had existed for Bachelors Grove Cemetery since the 1860s and likely after 1864, when the first homesteaders on the land—the Everdens—sold the property. It was probably at this time that the first survey and ownership of the lots was worked out. We have no idea at this time if the land was sold to the trustees by the Everdens or if ownership of graves was simply "claimed" by locals. It's possible that the Everdens actually sold or transferred the cemetery to the future board of trustees in a separate, unofficial transaction, but there are no legal records of such a transaction or even of an official board establishment or proceedings. At one point a Fulton family member said his family had purchased part of the cemetery at one time, but we don't know if he was referring to the Fulton lots or to a larger acreage. Possibly, the Fultons purchased the unused cemetery land from the Everdens and went on to sell the remaining parcels as needed and use the revenues for upkeep.

At any rate, the board included members of the Fulton family. Clarence Fulton was the most outspoken—and increasingly active and angry—advocate of the cemetery. Serving in midcentury, after the homesteaders left the land, he took his job very seriously, going so far as to hide in the cemetery at night with a colleague, with a gun, to chase away trespassers. The gun was taken away by police one night, however, after the pair fired three warning shots in the air during a scuffle with visitors.

As we've seen, by 1959, vandals were not only doing regular damage to tombstones but actually digging up graves. Reports were allegedly made by the trustees to Dan Ryan of the Forest Preserve District, but those reports have not yet been discovered in FPD archives. According to a 1959 newspaper report found in the clippings files of the Tinley Park Historical Society (from a column entitled All Points Southwest in an unknown publication), the Forest Preserve District had responded by building a gate across the cemetery entrance, which at the time apparently had some sort of fence around the enclosure. The gate was

> *14 feet long, six feet high, built of heavy galvanized pipe, some of it six inches in diameter. It was bolted, welded and constructed like the sides of a bridge. It weighed nearly 500 pounds. This jail-like frame was swung across the cemetery and kept shut by the use of a heavy chain, appropriately held together by a huge Yale snap lock.*

On Halloween night 1959, unknown pranksters used road flares to direct traffic from the Midlothian Turnpike into the cemetery:

> *Squads from the sheriff's police and the nearby state police headquarters sped to the cemetery, which shortly became jammed with cars, trucks, police cars and curiosity seekers attracted by the commotion and red police lights blinking among the dead....It was then that the big discovery was made: While all the commotion was going on in the cemetery, someone or something had swung the big gate shut and snapped a new and strong lock through the links of the big sturdy chain. There they were, state and county police, throngs of persons and scores of cars, securely locked up in the cemetery.*

A locksmith was sent for, who used a blowtorch to remove the chain and lock, and everyone dispersed. In the weeks that followed, a rigorous program of caretaking ensued, with plainclothes officers assigned to watch over the cemetery day and night, in search of the culprit or culprits who had staged the incident. Day after day, night after night, officers came away empty handed.

Then, on a brisk Monday morning in December, two months after the prank, forest preserve workers found that the five-hundred-pound cemetery gate had been stolen. Sometime between midnight and 5:00 a.m., it had simply disappeared.

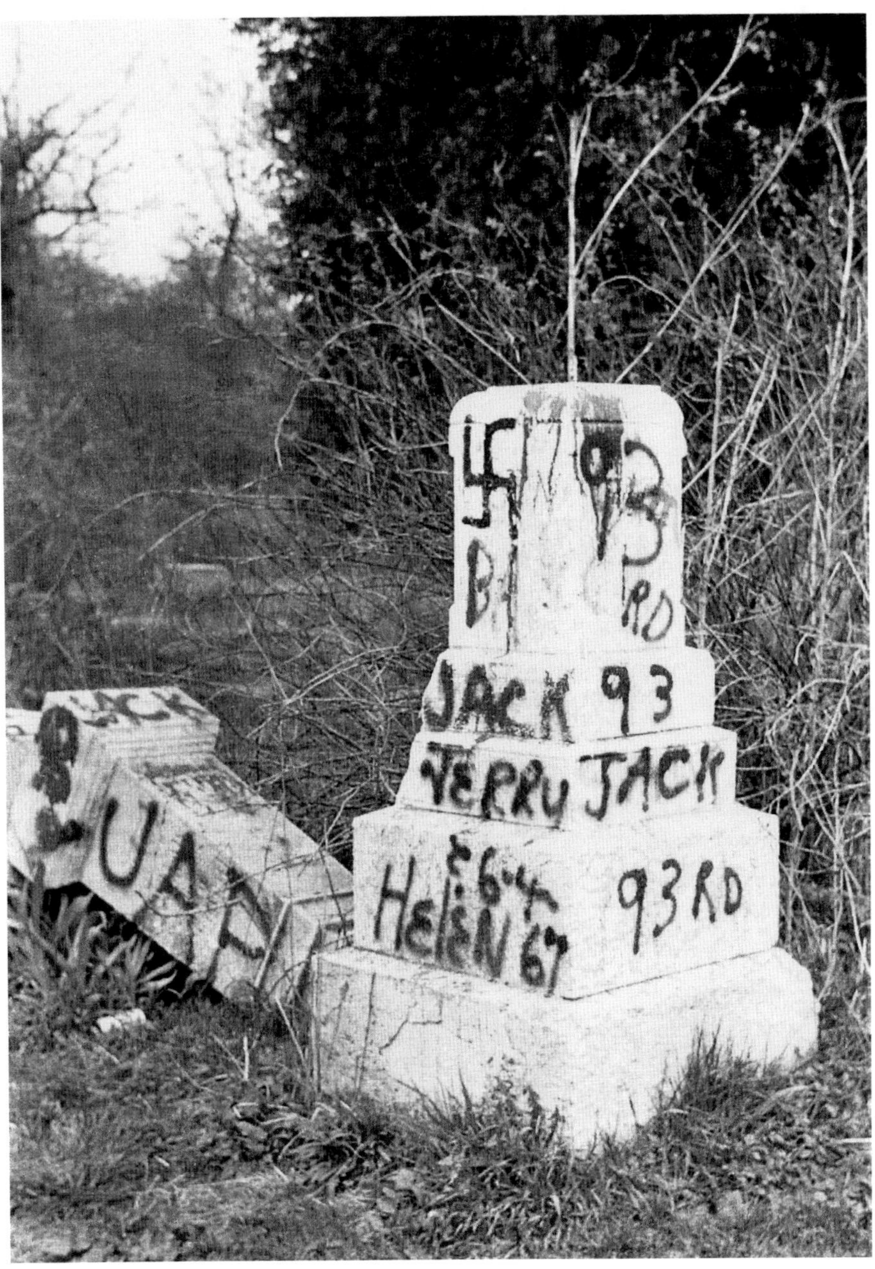

Vandalism at Bachelors Grove reached its peak in the 1960s and '70s, when graffiti, theft of headstones and monuments and even the digging up of graves had become regular occurrences. Local efforts of citizens to advocate for Bachelors Grove led to its condemnation in 1976 and a battle of wills between the county and unknown deviants that still rages today. *Ken Pursley.*

Police told reporters they were "perplexed."

Despite the efforts of the trustees, law-enforcement officials, forest preserve workers and local guardians, vandalism and theft of stones continued, with some of the worst damage occurring from 1969 to 1971. In 1969, Clarence Fulton reportedly petitioned Bremen Township to build a better fence around the cemetery and pay for caretaking services, both of which were denied by officials.

In 1972, Mark Preston, a senior at Bremen High School, wrote a letter to the editor of the local *Star Tribune*, noting the swift desecration and destruction of the cemetery, while also sharing the news that "Congressman Edward J. Derwinski, state Senator-elect Don Moore, local civic and historic groups, and the ancient Bachelors Grove Trustees association, have been laboring together to save and preserve the old cemetery." According to records he found, Preston said the cemetery is legally "non-existent," sharing with readers the contention of the state that the cemetery, having never been officially dedicated, could claim no legal standing as one; so, obtaining status as a state historical site was impossible.

Preston's efforts were part of a project that had been initiated by his teacher, Earnest Wilkinson, and the project grew into the Bremen High School Bicentennial Project of 1976, which gathered the most comprehensive information about the cemetery and the settlement up to the time and provided the foundation for future researchers to carry it forward.

Wilksinson's work, and that of his students, may have been the crucial element that led to a forcing of action as far as ownership of the cemetery. By 1977, plans were in motion by the county to do something about the disturbing activity at Bachelors Grove Cemetery. The *Suburban Tribune* reported on the plan on July 6, 1977:

> *The Cook County Cemetery trustees, a group formed by the county to oversee seven old cemeteries under county control, is planning to rehabilitate and protect Bachelor Grove Cemetery by the end of this summer. In the next two weeks, the county forest preserve district is expected to build a barrier at the entrance of a dirt road to the cemetery to keep cars out. Once that is done, a 7 foot high chain link fence with an additional foot of barbed wire at the top will be erected around the cemetery. Overturned headstones will be put back in their right places. The extensive work of vandals will be erased and the grounds will be put in good order. Thus promised Michael Igoe, then chairman of the trustees.*

23 653 514

LIS PENDENS NOTICE

IN THE CIRCUIT COURT OF COOK COUNTY ILLINOIS

THE COUNTY OF COOK, Petitioner

76L19294

vs. Case No.

EDWARD M. EVERDEN, et al., Defendant

BatchelorGrove Cemetery

I, the undersigned, do hereby certify that the above entitled cause was filed in the above Court on the 22 day of October 1976 for CONDEMNATION (Kind of Action) and is now pending in said Court and that the property affected by said cause is described as follows: (Give legal description): See Attached Sheet in Cook County, Illinois

Signature: MERCER COOK, Assistant State's Attorney (Type or print name for clarification) 1020 County Building, Chicago, Illinois 60602 (Address)

(Check one) ☐ Party to said Cause. ☒ Attorney of Record.

Mail to: Name / Address / or Deposit in Box No. ___ Recorder's Office.

NO CHARGE WILL CALL.

23653514

The condemnation of Bachelors Grove in 1976 ended its "orphaned" status and placed its ownership in the hands of Cook County, bringing to a close more than a century of private ownership and maintenance. *Tinley Park Historical Society.*

The year before, Bachelors Grove Cemetery had been declared "condemned"; that is, it was declared to be the property of the government—in this case, Cook County. Amazingly, half a century after the county had removed the homesteaders, the county had utilized the same legal means—a condemnation lawsuit—to take over the cemetery these men and women had left behind. In a moment, one of the oldest privately owned cemeteries in the nation—which had been cared for over more than a century by a private board—passed forever into the hands of the government.

Clarence Fulton's disgust was now complete. "They just stole it," he told the reporter. "I don't have anything to say any more." At this time, we don't know if there were negotiations between Fulton's trustees and the county before the condemnation was complete. Legal records have not yet been found. If there were, Fulton may have already been too despondent, and too tired, to care. By 1976, Fulton had already gone on record as deeply frustrated and angry about the lack of funds and energy he had to continue his mission to protect Bachelors Grove Cemetery. In the past decade he had gotten call after call from the police departments of Evergreen Park and Maywood, and even from Chicago Police headquarters, informing him that they had tombstones in their stations that had been stolen by vandals from Bachelors Grove. He finally told police to keep them, despairing that "if I bring them back here, they'll steal them again."

Bachelors Grove Cemetery was now owned by a branch of the slick, busy governmental agency also responsible for every county-owned building in Chicago. The Forest Preserve District no longer had any governing or

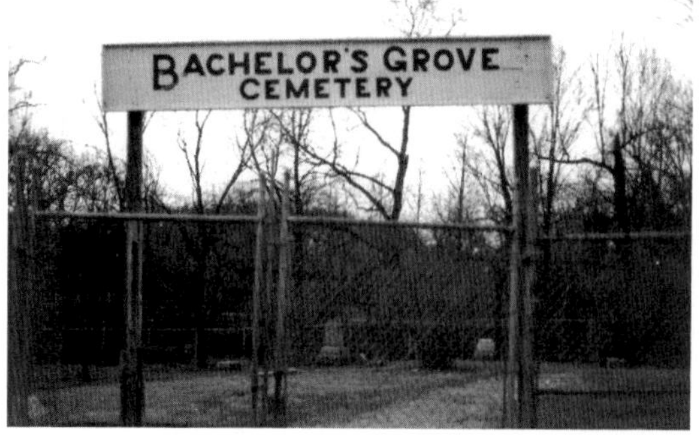

After the condemnation of the cemetery, the county installed a new fence and locked gate in 1977, but vandals soon found their way in to continue their destruction. The sign shown here in the late 1970s was toppled by the fall of 1982. *Dale Kaczmarek.*

maintenance interest in it, and the county made that clear when, just as Igoe had promised, the board installed a chain-link, barbed-wire-topped fence around the perimeter, separating it from the forest preserve land and declaring it "private property."

One morning not long after, Forest Preserve District workers reported that openings had been cut in the fence by trespassers, beer bottles and trash left behind and a heavy marker dragged halfway from its base to the quarry pond.

For the county, taking control of Bachelors Grove Cemetery was not going to be that easy.

6

BACHELORS GROVE TODAY

Today, the area known as Bachelors Grove is not the sprawling, multi-town area it was once known as but is generally held to be the forested area immediately surrounding the one-acre enclosure of Bachelors Grove Cemetery. This area covers no more than four square miles between Central and Ridgeland Avenues (east and west) and 147th Street to the part of 143rd Street known as the "new" Midlothian Turnpike. The south end opens up into an athletic field also operated by the Forest Preserve District of Cook County, and across the road is Chicago Gaelic Park, the area's massive Irish American heritage center and soccer fields. Nearby is the revered Midlothian Country Club and Camp Sullivan, an old Boy Scout camp that has been newly rehabbed for general public use.

Currently, Bachelors Grove Cemetery is reportedly owned by the Real Estate Management Office of Cook County, but today the administration of it is a loose cooperation between the office and the Forest Preserve District. Organized tours and other large gatherings must arrange a permit through the FPD, and cemetery visitors must abide by the same rules as preserve visitors: sunrise to sunset only. The county makes it clear, however, that the cemetery is not public land like the preserve around it. It is private property (inasmuch as county land can be), presumably covering its bases in the event of any incidents.

It is unclear what happened to the county cemetery trustees, or even if such a board still exists. Certainly, in recent years Cook County and its government have been very much in the news regarding cemeteries and burials. In 2009, Burr Oak Cemetery in neighboring Alsip was declared a crime scene by Sheriff Tom Dart after a horrific scandal came to light: workers had been reselling graves for years, dumping bodies in mass graves and reselling plots for cash. Cook County Board president Toni Preckwinkle and head medical examiner Nancy Jones were taken to task in 2012 when it was discovered that dozens of unidentified bodies of indigent county residents had piled up in the county morgue over an unknown period of time. And throughout the 1990s and beyond, the county was under fire for its part in the baffling situation at Chicago State Hospital (Dunning Asylum), where it is believed that more than thirty-eight thousand bodies were "forgotten" after the hospital and adjoining poor farm were closed. Despite massive involvement in and obvious concern for the cemetery at nearby Oak Forest Hospital—now a carefully tended historic site—the creation of a memorial park for the dead of Dunning and the huge overhaul of laws in light of the Burr Oak Cemetery scandal, the presence of the county at Bachelors Grove seems essentially nonexistent.

Since the condemnation suit in 1976 and its stalled plan to "fix" Bachelors Grove, numerous efforts have been initiated by private citizens and organizations to repair and replace the stones at the cemetery, have Bachelors Grove Cemetery declared a historic site and figure out some plan for securing its future. Endless cleanups have been hosted by volunteers; websites built to flesh out and save its history; petitions created and circulated; and picnics, lectures, exhibits and tours held to raise awareness. Many decades after Mark Preston's efforts, the nearly fifteen-year efforts of another independent advocate, Peter Crapia from nearby Palos Hills, were reportedly met with similar roadblocks, with governmental agencies informing him that since there was no historic building or structure on the site, Bachelors Grove Cemetery did not qualify for historic designation. During the same time, he and another local resident built separate, detailed websites devoted to the history of Bachelors Grove, both of which drew hundreds of visitors to not only their online forums but also numerous cleanup and tour outings to the cemetery. Between 2012 and 2014, a cemetery restoration expert from central Illinois showed interest in restoring the cemetery through the Illinois Historic Preservation Agency, but efforts were abandoned by either her, the state or the county for unknown reasons.

Bachelors Grove today, then, exists as an anomaly in and of itself, aside from its world-famous, anomalous phenomena. Though numerous people and groups have tirelessly labored for its heritage and well-being, the public is kept essentially in the dark about its governance and maintenance—and its future. Even the respected local historians who would ordinarily be the natural advocates and supporters of real change have an often hostile relationship with the advocates of Bachelors Grove, who understandably feel that any additional attention to the cemetery will just add to its further desecration.

All that's left, then, is for advocates to love this place and to look after it as best they can, while they wait for the government to decide its fate. And so, as they have done for generations, those attracted to this place make the sometimes long trek here, by the thousands each year, in any weather, with friends or family or alone. They park their cars, cross the new turnpike road and step inside….

THE PATH

Most visitors approach Bachelors Grove Cemetery from the north end of the surrounding woods, where the new turnpike meets the old, as the official parking area for the cemetery woods is in the Rubio Woods lot off the new 143rd Street Midlothian Turnpike (no vehicle traffic is allowed on the old road). It is in this lot that local hearse clubs sometimes display their vehicles, where tour groups rendezvous and where loose organizations of Bachelors Grove "fans" congregate. There are two other ways in. One is by a vague footpath off Central Avenue and 143rd Street, behind a smattering of private homes. The other is from the athletic field on 147th Street. Be warned that you really must know where you are going if you use either of these routes, even legitimately and legally in daylight hours. As naturalist Joe Cavataio emphasizes in his essay in this book, Bachelors Grove's landscape is extremely tricky to navigate, and the density of buckthorn makes it easy to get cut off from seeing roads, houses or even nearby footpaths.

It's even tricky to get in the "front" door. Visitors must cross the busy and dangerous new turnpike road by foot to access the old Midlothian Turnpike, today generally referred to as "the Path," a somewhat narrow old road of broken concrete that leads past the cemetery entrance a quarter mile through the woods. Across the path entrance stands a forest preserve gate, locked against car access by a secured cable, and metal signs that read "Closed" and "Closed at Sunset." These have been repeatedly stolen, presumably by souvenir hunters. Just inside the entrance one may still see the old gate post foundations, reminders of a larger gate that once stood here at some unknown time.

This path, we shall see, is a big part of the stage for Bachelors Grove's strange phenomena. Visitors find themselves surrounded by natural beauty and by a sense often described as "magical" or "enchanted." This feeling is regularly enhanced by paranormal experiences: seeing phantom dogs or houses, hearing voices or footsteps, being lured into the woods by hypnotic lights or being pelted with objects by unseen hands. Recall that this was originally a Native American trail and then the old Midlothian Turnpike, the Old Blue Island Road that was a main public highway until the 1920s. Among the many who used this road were soldiers who marched on it to reach Blue Island and board trains, headed for duty during the American Civil War. Some investigators believe that at least a portion of activity experienced on this path is from residual energy left by the many travelers on this road over a very long period of time.

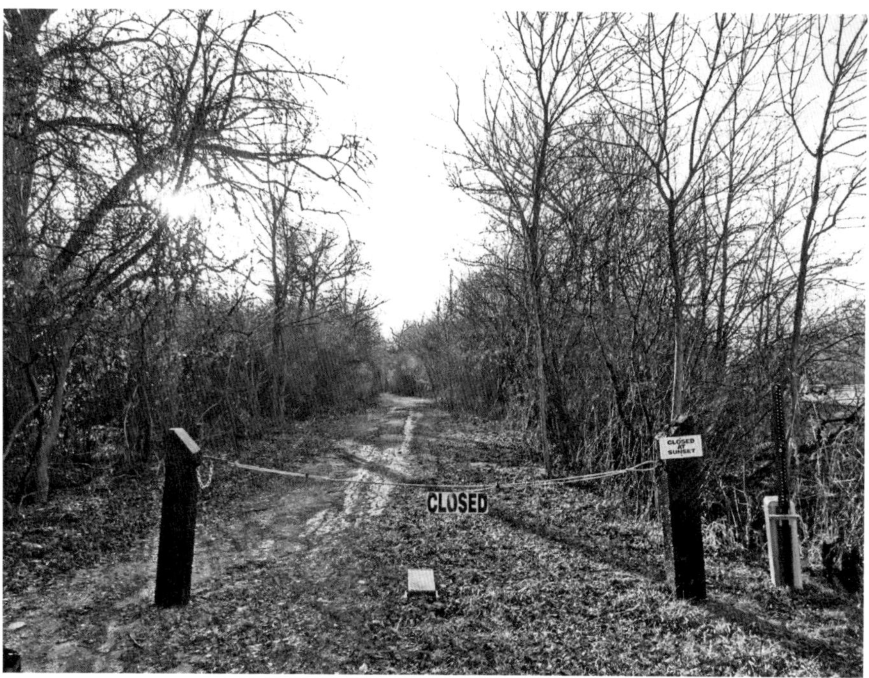

A cable and post gate today bars vehicle access to the old Midlothian Turnpike, known today as the path to Bachelors Grove. The broken road, flanked by forest, is traversed by thousands of curiosity seekers each year, in search of the enigmatic burying ground about a quarter mile down its stretch. *Karl K.*

Others believe there may be some sort of time anomaly here, where sounds from another dimension somehow overflow into ours.

Dr. Chuck Kennedy, a longtime paranormal researcher from the area, was at Bachelors Grove in 2012 with a friend, recording for electronic voice phenomenon (EVP) with a very sensitive parabolic microphone. While they had the device aimed toward the path, past the front gate, the pair recorded what sounded like troops marching. That same year, Zak Bagans—host of television's *Ghost Adventures*—visited the Grove and wondered if the pieces of broken road itself may contain residual energy from travelers who used it during the twentieth century.

Bill Swinford, a local resident, heard what sounded like a car door slamming on the path just outside the cemetery gate. He was at the time talking with someone and recalls that the person turned in the direction when it sounded again. When Swinford asked if he heard something, he said, "Yeah, it was a car door."

Paranormal or not, the walk along the path to the woods can be dangerous for some due to the broken pavement and especially in winter, when no plowing is done here and snow can be deep and ice tricky to navigate.

THE WOODS

Most of the acreage surrounding Bachelors Grove Cemetery is not natural forest. Most of this area was—like much of the Chicago area—swampy prairie and scattered timber stands when it was first squatted upon by those early New Englanders who harvested the grove timber here. After these first arrivals moved on to Blue Island and elsewhere to marry and settle down, farms were cultivated here; mid-nineteenth-century maps show a thriving farming community covered with family farms and homesteads, with the timber grove still intact nearby.

Today, the woods surrounding Bachelors Grove Cemetery are filled with plant life, including a wide variety of trees, a contagion of buckthorn, the wild onion or *checagou* that gave Chicago its name and the endless twines of immensely thorny brambles that seem to wrap around one's ankles like a scene from a children's tale. Very little removal is done in these woods, leaving a somewhat precarious expanse, including many dead trees waiting to take their final bow. In most seasons, standing still, one may hear them creaking, which some visitors mistake for rusty doors on the area's famed phantom farmhouse.

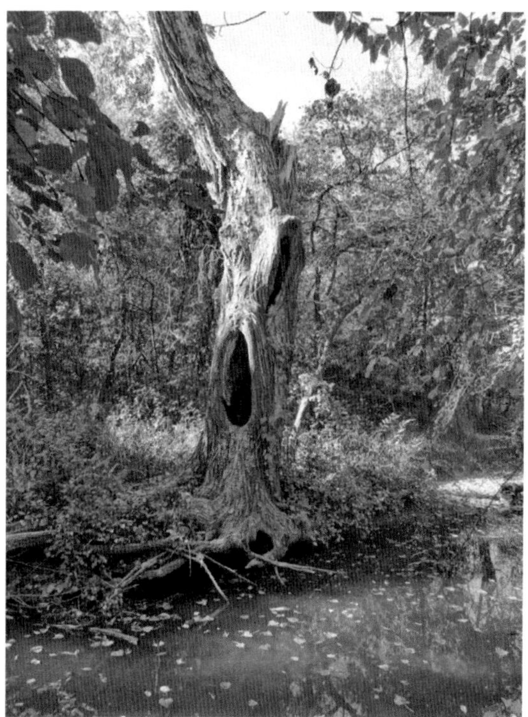

The re-forested area surrounding Bachelors Grove Cemetery is known today as Everden Woods. Part of the Rubio Woods Forest Preserve, the environs are filled with curious landmarks, such as the "Holy Tree," also known as "Spooky Tree," for obvious reasons. *Karl K.*

The woods are strewn with the remains of several homesteads and farms, which are points of pilgrimage for visitors to the area, who make a game of finding them all and boast when they do. Having found them all is a status symbol among regular visitors—a sign that one is a real aficionado of the Grove. Though it's difficult to pinpoint the identity of these sites, there are three that have been pretty definitely identified. One is the remains of the homestead of the Frederich Schmidt family, the last family to live in these woods. In early spring, before much growth, the clear remains of the home may still be seen near the entrance to the Grove not far from the old turnpike road: shards of broken crockery and bottles, pieces of roofing tile, broken bricks and tools, shoe leather and the sunken foundation of the home itself. A well or cistern is still visible behind the house property as well. Across the creek are the remains of what was likely the home of Albert Hardy, who came to Bremen Township from Liverpool in the nineteenth century—and whose mother, Edna Wright Hardy Sanderson, is buried at Bachelors Grove. Another homesite that we know of for sure is that of Christian Boehm, who created the quarry and lived on the ravine just west of it; but, according to legal records, the home had no foundation and no well or cistern and so left no trace after its removal. There are other foundations and even a silo in the woods, but at this time it is difficult to say for sure whose properties these structures marked.

Like many of the forest preserves of Cook County, the woods around Bachelors Grove Cemetery have long been a place of refuge for the homeless, the displaced and the disenfranchised, beginning in the early days of the preserves. During the Great Depression, many of the forest preserves were utilized as places of refuge by the homeless, mostly men, without work or shelter. Makeshift shelters were created with some frequency. Today, this practice continues again in many of the larger county preserves, despite law-enforcement efforts to quell it. Hikers still find lean-tos and other shelters in the woods surrounding Bachelors Grove, as well as the remains of camps such as firepits, clothing and food cans and boxes.

Also here, later in the century, another form of refuge was provided by the sheltering trees: a place of retreat for patients at nearby Oak Forest Hospital, an infirmary for the mentally ill, now closed. According to a lifetime resident of the area, well into the late twentieth century, patients would regularly spend their weekend "good behavior" passes in the woods at Bachelors Grove and other local preserves, preferring the beauty and peace of the preserves to that of their family homes. Others had nowhere else to go but didn't want to give up their passes. More than one man allegedly died of exposure during these outings.

Of course, many contemporary souls find the forest preserves a place of retreat from the "real world" today. Loners, outcasts and those who have separated themselves from mainstream society such as artists, musicians and alternative religious practitioners, especially nature-based ones, such as Wiccans and Druids, will often be found "hanging out" in the preserves.

For Chicago-area teenagers, the forest preserves have since their inception been a place of retreat from family and school life, in these liminal spaces removed from the "real world." From the kids of the country club set who bothered Hubert Geist in the 1930s to the "partiers" and "stoners" of the 1970s and beyond, the forest preserves have played a big part in the social and cultural lives of Chicago's young people.

I will never forget something that a colleague said to me one summer afternoon after many afternoons spent at Bachelors Grove together: "I love to see you here," he said. "You are younger and not worried about anything." Ask any south-side Chicagoan of middle age, and they will tell you the same thing about their youth: the preserves were their place of refuge from the real world. This was their own world, a place where even high school cliques dissolved.

Parapsychologist George Hanson believes that this very liminality plays a big part in paranormal experience. When we cross over into a different world from the one we know, Hanson says, we tend to be more open to paranormal experience. This is why tourists or new residents tend to have anomalous experiences at locations where longtime residents have had none. That the preserves continue to offer this sort of escape for people cannot be ignored by those seeking the roots of the experiences at Bachelors Grove.

The isolation and shelter of the Cook County preserves have also been used for deviant purposes. In recent decades, a growing phenomenon in most of the Cook County forest preserves has been the prevalence of visitors seeking anonymous, usually homosexual "hook ups" or liaisons in the woods. The woods surrounding Bachelors Grove have been part of this trend for decades. A local resident remembers hanging out in the area in the 1980s and being warned about the "creepers" or "cruisers" who would drive up and down Batchelor Grove Road (now gone) looking for young men:

> *Guys would cruise it looking for...other guys. At Carlson Springs Woods there is a rectangular shaped pit, made of stones, water drains into it. In the '80s we frequented the woods. Carlson Springs was a cool place because it was right next to Tinley Creek. The Creepers, as we called them, they used to say, "Hey, that's Gacy's bathtub."* [John Wayne Gacy was a Chicago-area serial killer who killed more than thirty young men before his arrest in December 1979.]

An awareness of these activities is important for those studying the paranormal aspects of Bachelors Grove, as some occult practitioners believe that sexual acts may release powerful energies into an area that can linger for a long while. Some occult traditions even try to tap into these energies during spellcasting or the practice of "magick." It's possible, then, that rampant sexual activity may have been a big factor in drawing occultists here for the practice of their rituals.

The Forest Preserve District of Cook County wages an ongoing battle against the practice of ritual activity in the preserves, many of which have earned a well-deserved reputation over the years as sites rife with "Satanic" or other such practices. Such incidents have included documented reports of animal sacrifice, claims of human sacrifice and suicides and homicides believed to be tied to ritualistic—often Satanic—practices or beliefs. For generations, law-enforcement officers and officials have verified claims made by many visitors to Rubio Woods that the butchered remains of dogs, chickens and other small animals in the woods testify to such activities. Pentagrams drawn in chalk in clearings and reports of hooded figures and ritualistic chanting: all seem to point to the reality of many of the reports.

A nearby neighbor went on record as recently as the 2000s claiming that his chickens had been stolen and found dead and mutilated in the cemetery.

On September 26, 1989, the *Chicago Tribune* published a disturbing article that featured an interview with Craig Tisdale, an animal control officer who specialized in cult-related animal abuse cases. Tisdale discussed the growing problem of cult activity in the forest preserves and the very real possibility of human—and even infant—sacrifice in the Cook County preserves. Tisdale shared that "most of the forest sites are being used principally by teenagers and young adults who are experimenting with the occult." The officer talked about the telltale signs: animal carcasses, red candle wax and other evidence familiar to Bachelors Grove visitors. He also talked about the conditions that make the preserves so hospitable to cult activity. As naturalist Joe Cavataio also points out, Tisdale referenced the natural growth (like the buckthorn so prevalent at places like Bachelors Grove) as an excellent cover for illicit or criminal activity.

Also reported at the Grove have been tripwires or fishing line found stretched across paths in the woods, something Tisdale said was common at sites of ritual activity because of massive efforts to keep observers and meddlers away at any cost: "They are booby-trapped with Vietnam-like pungi stakes or spikes hammered through planks. There are trip wires and neck wires to knock you down."

THE CEMETERY

Approaching Bachelors Grove Cemetery from the path, it comes up quickly, its chain-link fence looming to the north. Most visitors are startled to lay eyes on the cemetery after hearing of its reputation. The tiny enclave at first barely resembles a cemetery and certainly not one of such harrowing repute. But upon closer inspection, the sadness seeps in.

Most of the headstones have been stolen or destroyed or long decayed, leaving a largely vacant expanse. Fewer than two dozen remain. Naturally, those that do have taken on iconic proportions for fans of the cemetery, and they are easily recognized by their shape and known by their family names: the Fulton stone, the Shields stone, the Hageman stone, the Moss stone, the

Patrick stone, the Deck stone, the Newman stone, the Hamilton stone. Some of these are not markers at all but the bases that remain after the theft of the rest of the pieces. Most of the markers and bases are made of limestone or granite. Few have more than simple names and dates engraved upon them, many worn away forever.

In recent years, the county sent a cleanup crew through the cemetery to remove much of the overgrowth of flora for which the burial ground was famous. Once upon a time, this cemetery was famed for its flowers and trees: hundreds of lilies and other flowers would cover the grounds, flanked by rose bushes and other shrubs and stately oak, cedars and other mature trees. After the private trustees left, the lushness of nature took over, and in high summer, Illinois prairie flowers and grass were commonly waist high, blotting out most of the cemetery monuments. In September, a froth of snowy blooms turned the enclave into a sea of white. Vines literally covered the trunks of the standing trees, and daylilies and periwinkle, long ago planted by kind visitors, helped to buoy the fragile stones. Since the "cleanup" (and the apparent scrapping of the most recent restoration plans), dangerous and quick erosion has threatened the remaining standing stones, soil washing away at alarming rates with the spring rains, and one whole perimeter stretch threatens to cave in at any moment. The flood of 2013 added insult to injury. The Fulton stone, in particular, was already being reinforced by visitors who would wedge small rocks and pieces of broken concrete underneath the base stone to stave off inevitable instability. After the flooding and erosion of the last few years, one visitor reinforced the base with stones and dirt.

The Quarry and the Creek

Just past the Fulton stone, beyond the stretch of fence, lies the old quarry, now filled with dark water, which hosts a famously bright green covering of duckweed in the summer. Local legend suggests that many of the cemetery's missing headstones may lie at the quarry floor. In fact, one stone was hauled up close to shore by a group of volunteers in the early 2000s. Some have lived in hope that the county would drain the quarry and discover the rumored remains at the bottom: automobiles, missing tombstones, ploughs, bodies and other whispered artifacts of legends past—as well as the true dimensions of it.

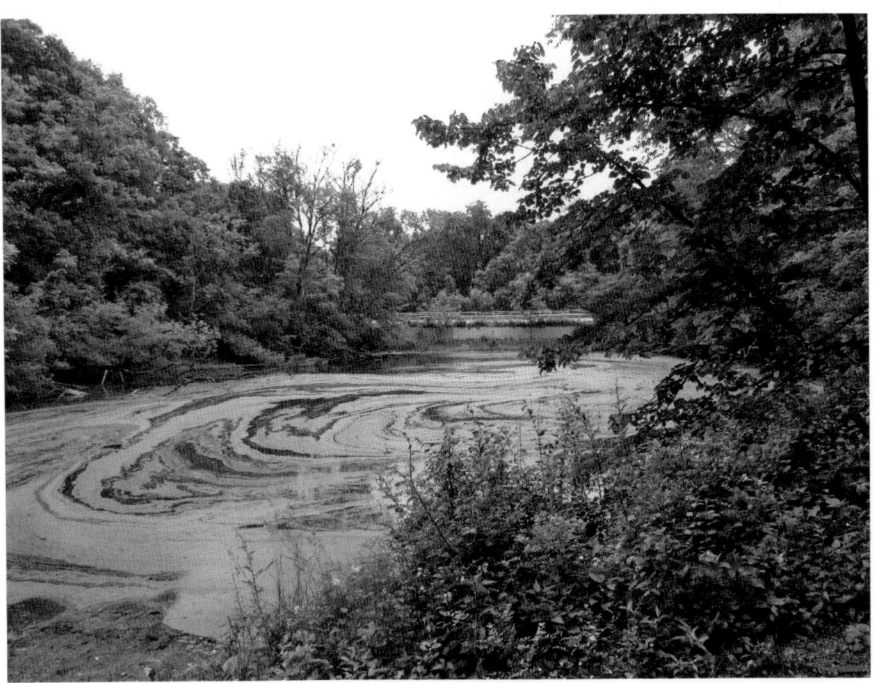

The Bachelors Grove pond is actually a water-filled quarry, which was opened by Christian Boehm in 1909 on land deeded to his father, Frederick, by the Schmidt family. When the Schmidts sold the forest preserve land, the sale excluded not only the cemetery but the quarry land as well. The quarry is the site and source of many of Bachelors Grove's ghost stories. Its dark surface, in summer covered with a bright green coat of duckweed, is said to hide many secrets. *Karl K.*

One paranormal investigator, Dr. Chuck Kennedy, sent down a device of his own invention to record sound and video under water and verified depths of at least fifty feet. However, other observers have claimed that the pond is shallow. In a recent summer, one local resident watched a young boy hunting toads and reported that he walked all the way across and reported a depth of six feet at most. However, quarries are known for their various and sudden depth changes, so unless divers are sent down to explore—or unless the pond is drained—the true dimensions and mysterious contents may never be known. Boating and swimming are forbidden in all but a few designated water features in the FPDCC, so probing the depth with weighted ropes or attempting to dive are off-limits as well as extremely dangerous. From the Boehm court hearing, the quarry is assumed to have been about twenty feet deep at the time of the hearing, but today, numerous factors may have made its depth very different.

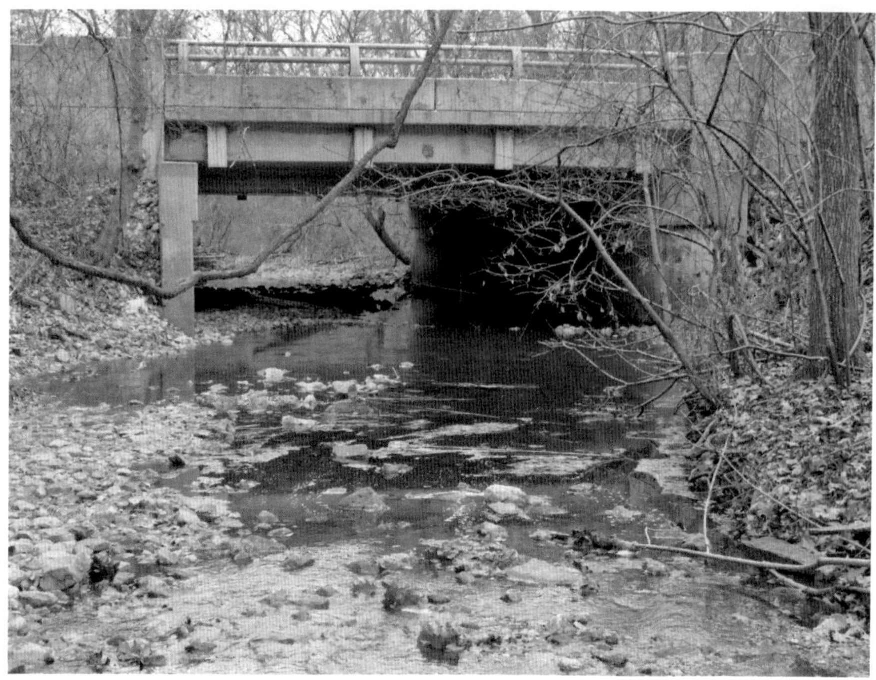

An artery of Tinley Creek (originally called Bachelors Grove Creek) runs through Everden Woods and past the western fence line of Bachelors Grove Cemetery, under the new turnpike road at 143rd Street. In its thriving days, numerous bridges spanned the creek to provide ease of travel for area residents. Today, they have all disappeared. Artifacts found in the creek over the years have provided clues to the past of this mysterious place. *Karl K.*

Just west of the cemetery and quarry is a drainage artery of the Tinley Creek, originally called Bachelors Grove Creek, which runs all the way through Everden Woods. When this was farmland, there were bridges crossing the creek at the turnpike road and at other points throughout the acreage where homesteads once stood. Today, there are no bridges still standing. Hikers generally cross the creek across the rocks of the creek bed, where a footpath dips down from the path—the turnpike road—west of the cemetery. Be warned: it's wet and slippery, and the paths around it are often mucky. The creek can also still be dangerously high, especially in spring with the seasonal rains.

THE LOTS AND THE STONES

There are 82 lots at Bachelors Grove Cemetery. Historians have in the past estimated that there were between 135 and 200 burials in the cemetery between 1838 and 1989. Unfortunately, again, there are no known burial records for Bachelors Grove Cemetery. The only known notations made by the trustees were of ownership or transfers of the lots, and these only beginning after 1860, more than two decades after the first known burials. Therefore, creating a picture of the actual interments (also taking into account the possibility of undiscovered re-interments) is, in short, a pretty much impossible task. Heroic attempts to make sense of the situation were made twice before. First, Bremen High School students and teachers read the stones and researched the graves as part of their Bicentennial History Project of 1976. As stated, at least one of the students, Mark Preston, came to believe that the cemetery is older than has been believed, possibly dating to 1832 or even earlier.

In 1994, Tinley Park historian Brad Bettenhausen published a heroic lot breakdown of the cemetery, listing all known information about the burials. Unfortunately, the excellent, detailed diagram that was produced from this effort has been widely misinterpreted. Many lot notations indicating ownership or sales have been interpreted as actual burial records on Internet cemetery record sites, which in turn have been utilized by family historians spreading the misinformation through ancestry and genealogy sites. Often, it seems, these lots were transferred or abandoned altogether, as the original owners went on to other settlement areas, and yet the original owners are frequently listed as interred at Bachelors Grove.

For the past several years, Bachelors Grove historian Wendy Moxley Roe and I have separately and together attempted to track down as much actual burial documentation as possible, in order to present a more accurate picture of the interments at the Grove. Starting with Mr. Bettenhausen's record and incorporating county vital records, funeral home registries, obituaries and other newspaper articles and public and private family trees, we offer the current state of the project at the end of this volume, as Appendix B.

Though many of the graves around the perimeter of the cemetery are listed on the ownership map as "Unsold," and presumably empty, in the spring of 2016 we surveyed the cemetery with dowsing rods and confirmed dozens of additional burials in these "unsold" lots. Many of the lots seem to actually be full, containing nine or more burials. There is literally no way of knowing the occupants of these graves, unless a burial registry surfaces in the

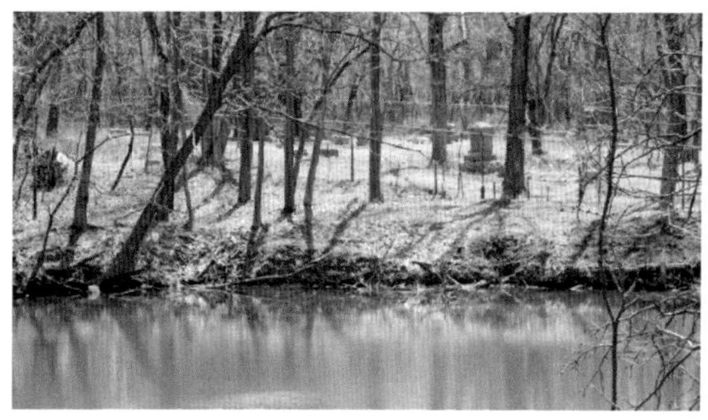

Bachelors Grove as seen from across the old quarry pond from the new 143rd Street Turnpike viaduct. *Author's collection.*

future. One possibility is that these perimeter lots were reserved as paupers' graves, of which more later. We also confirmed that there were several burials outside of the modern fence, at least to the south and west. Whether these burials are part of known lots or occurred outside of the cemetery for religious or legal cultural reasons is uncertain at this time. With the additional findings, and presuming no unknown re-interments, this would put the burials at Bachelors Grove at over 170 persons and possibly as many as 200 or more. Despite the numbers, there are fewer than 20 headstones, markers or bases remaining today. It is highly probable that many graves were never marked or only marked with wooden markers, uninscribed rocks or saplings, such as those of the twin cedar trees that still stand today.

Entering the cemetery from the old turnpike road and the southeast quadrant (to the right), the visitor encounters the largest grouping of stones in the burying ground. These are also the earliest burials. The remains of the markers nearest the entrance are believed to be the remnants of Fulton family stones, from the fence to the stone marked "Wheeler."

John Fulton Sr. and his wife, Jane Johnson, were both born in Ireland and immigrated to America in 1839. They made their way west to the bourgeoning Illinois lands outside Chicago, where they purchased eighty acres of the wooded area of Bremen Township known then as Bachelors Grove. The couple bore fourteen children on the farm they operated, and at the time of his death in 1883, John had become the most influential and respected of the area's citizens, owning more than one thousand acres of land, with his family closely tied to the administration of the community, as his descendants still are in Tinley Park today. The young couple were raising their family in the recent "Indian lands" of the Illinois wilds, and local Native Americans would come each morning to the Fulton farm for milk, often returning after the day's hunt with a cut of deer meat for Jane to prepare for the family. During the building of the Rock Island railroad, the Fultons boarded the workers for ten cents a day, including meals and lodging.

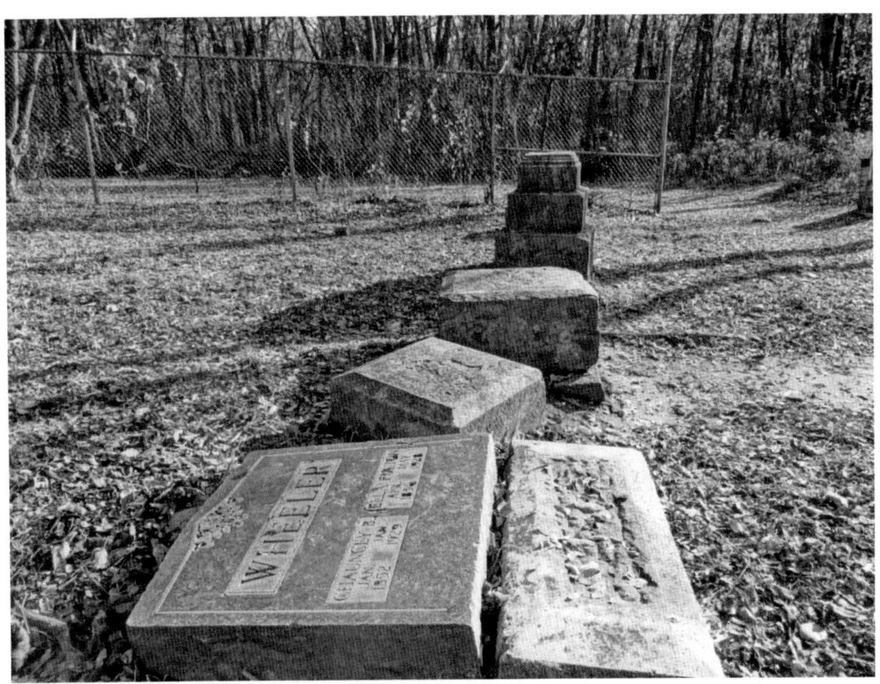

Monuments to the Fulton family stand near the cemetery entrance. One of the most influential families in Bremen Township even today, these rugged pioneers lived lives of enormous courage and tragedy. Many of them are interred at Bachelors Grove. *Wendy Moxley Roe.*

Two of John and Jane's children, Ella and Robert, are also interred here. According to local oral history, Robert committed suicide at the age of thirty-one by walking in front of a Rock Island train near present-day Tinley Park, sometime before 1935. Ella's husband, Chauncey Wheeler, also rests here with his wife, their graves marked by the Wheeler marker, often toppled. Amazingly, Joseph Fulton, born in the 1770s, is also interred here. He was the father of John Sr. and Hamilton Fulton. According to old records, a large white obelisk once stood here, reading:

Joseph Fulton, Died 15 Oct 1852 at the age of 80

Near the Fultons is the iconic "Moss" marker, which is only the base of a complete marker that once towered here. However, when family members found that the granite obelisk topping the base had been dragged nearly to the road, the marker was given into the care of the Tinley Park Historical

Society, cleaned and placed outside the society headquarters at the Old Landmark Church, where it may be seen today.

Thomas Moss's life, like that of many residents of the Grove, was often visited by death. His first wife, Isabella, died in 1848 after a thirteen-year marriage. The couple had seven children, two of whom were stillborn and two of whom died in childhood. After Isabella's death, Thomas married Sarah McGettingen, who passed away less than a year later. Two years later, Thomas wed again. His third wife, Anna Turney, was the sister of Hulda Turney Fulton, buried under the famed Fulton stone near the quarry pond. This third marriage produced seven more children, of whom one was stillborn and two died in infancy. Then, in 1885, Anna and her last child died in childbirth. Thomas never married again. Isabella is buried here with him.

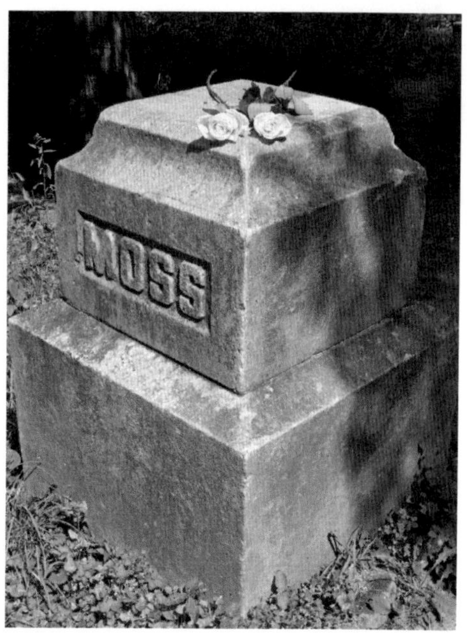

This marker on a lot belonging to the Moss family is one of the most iconic at Bachelors Grove. The tall granite top of the marker was found to have been dragged nearly to the road one day in the late 1970s, forcing the family to remove it for safekeeping. Today, it may be seen in the dooryard of the Tinley Park Historical Society at the Old Landmark Church. *Wendy Moxley Roe.*

Also in this quadrant are the lots of the Crandall family, now unmarked. The Crandall brothers were some of the most colorful characters in Cook County in its earliest days, well known in Chicago and not a little notorious. In 1833, Heman Crandall (sometimes called Herman in records), then twenty-one, left the shores of Lake Champlain in New York and walked more than eight hundred miles to Chicago. He also went back and forth on visits twice more—on foot. Two of his brothers, David and Mark, made the journey to Chicago by canoe, and at the first government land sale in Illinois, held at the Bull's Head tavern on Lake Michigan, the brothers purchased prairie lands in Bremen Township for $1.25 an acre. Some of the Crandalls went on to settle in present-day Worth, then called Lane's Island, building the first houses there. The Crandalls were typical of the very earliest settlers, who spent most of their lives not as farmers but as loggers, moving west with the expanding frontier. When he was sixty-nine years old, Ben Crandall went on to Nebraska, where he purchased a substantial tract of largely unimproved land, intending to divide it among his children. Returning later to Bremen Township, he continued to farm until his death in his late seventies. Mark Crandall's daughter Alma was only sixteen years old at the time of her death and burial at Bachelors Grove in 1870. His surviving daughter, Electa, lost her own daughter, Clara Webber, when the infant was only three weeks old. She was also buried at Bachelors Grove. Several of the Crandall family members interred at the Grove were reinterred at Mount Greenwood Cemetery in Chicago in 1895, on the same day. It is uncertain if any of the grave markers on the Crandall family lot at Mount Greenwood originally stood in Bachelors Grove. In 1935, however, at least one Crandall grave marker remained at the Grove: that of Alvah Crandall, who died in July 1843 at the age of thirty-nine. His stone was still present in 1935, when it was mentioned in a newspaper article. No re-interment records exist for Alvah. It is presumed he remains at the Grove.

Lot 43 is home to settler Richard Moss and family, including his wife, Maria, and their numerous children and spouses. There are three stones remaining, including Richard's headstone showing his name and dates. A landmark here on the lot until very recently was the "Split Tree," which was strangely beloved by visitors. Its double trunk was split almost to the ground for years. A friend of the Grove in its last year chained the trunks together, hoping to keep them from falling apart altogether. But county maintenance crews finally sawed them down to the stumps. Remaining at their base, however, are the twin markers of John McKee and Delaney Ann (Hulett) McKee. Born in 1854 to pioneer parents, Delaney Ann was a twenty-five-year veteran teacher in the Cook County schools, including at the famed Stone School at Bachelors Grove. She died in 1920.

Nearby is the lot of the Patrick family, which is home of the famed "moving tombstone"—one of the most recognizable stones at Bachelors Grove. One of the earliest known photos of Bachelors Grove Cemetery, which appeared in a local paper in 1951 and refers to the burial ground as "Smith's Cemetery" in the article, shows the stone had by then already moved from its appointed spot. Keep in mind that this was several years *after* vandalism began at the Grove, so one assumes that it was vandals (not spirits) who first began to move it. The Patrick family's most famous member was Amelia Patrick, who married Senator John Humphrey, whose "Humphrey House" historical museum still operates in Orland Park. Amelia and John's

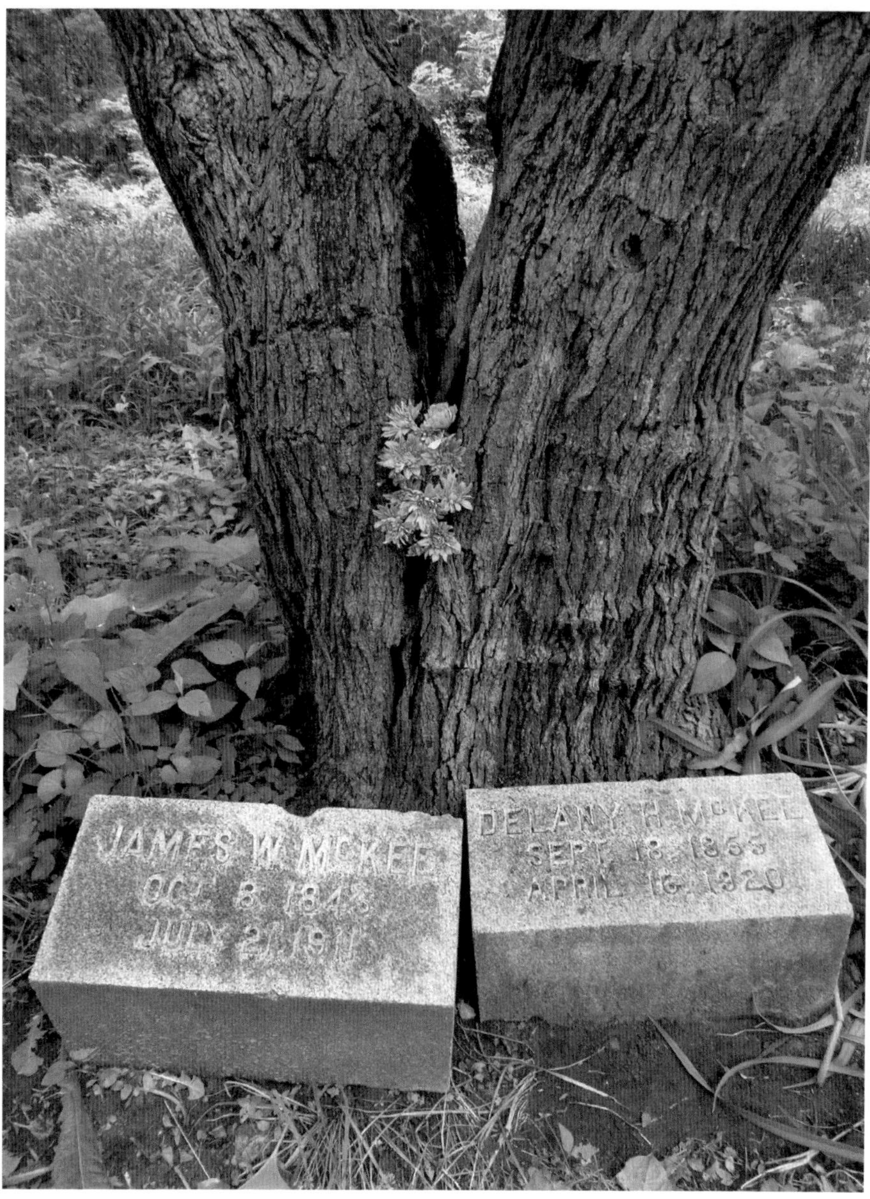

These twin headstones belonging to the McKee family have long stood at the base of the "split tree," now sawed down to a stump, in the cemetery's southeast quadrant. *Wendy Moxley Roe.*

infant daughter, Libby May Humphrey, rests at Bachelors Grove, where she and her mother are the source of much talk in paranormal circles, of which more later.

Past the cedar trees known as "The Pines" is the stone marking the Rippet family lot, which was last photographed upright in 1951. The Rippets were dairy farmers in Blue Island, and James Rippet was a Blue Island police officer. The farming members moved to Oregon, Illinois, later in life. In the very far corner of this quadrant is the lot marked by the stone of William Hamilton, whose identity is unknown. Though other Hamiltons are buried elsewhere in the cemetery, we do not at this time know if this is a relation, as burial records for a related William do not match up. This plot is, however, believed to be the burial site of the oldest known burial here—that of William B. Nobles in 1836. His marker is long gone.

Continuing north along the east fence wall, visitors can see the severe erosion that began after the flood of 2013, worsened by the recent removal of wild and cultivated plants that helped to curtail earlier erosion. Along the fence line of the northeast quadrant, the ground slopes dangerously down into a small stream of runoff water.

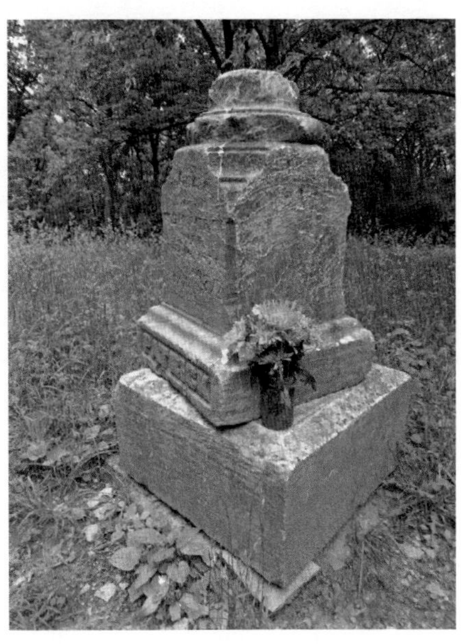

The famous "moving tombstone"—seen here out of place as usual—has been reported in every area of the cemetery since at least 1951, but it has never been removed from the grounds. It remains a favorite target of vandals or, some say, spirits. The stone originally marked the lot of the Patrick family, whose most famous member was Amelia Patrick, first wife of Senator John Humphrey. Their child, little Libby May Humphrey, was interred here after her infant death. *Wendy Moxley Roe.*

In this quadrant, visitors find the lots of the Deck family and the Shields family. Joseph and Jennie (Deck) Niklas were two of five family members killed in July 1921 when their car stalled on the tracks at 90th Street and Vincennes Avenue and was struck by a freight train. Jennie's parents, Jacob and Mary, and brother Bernard rest here as well.

Edna Wright Hardy Sanderson lies in an unmarked grave here at Bachelors Grove, alone. An English native, she bore seventeen children, several of whom came to Bremen Township to live. She visited Chicago

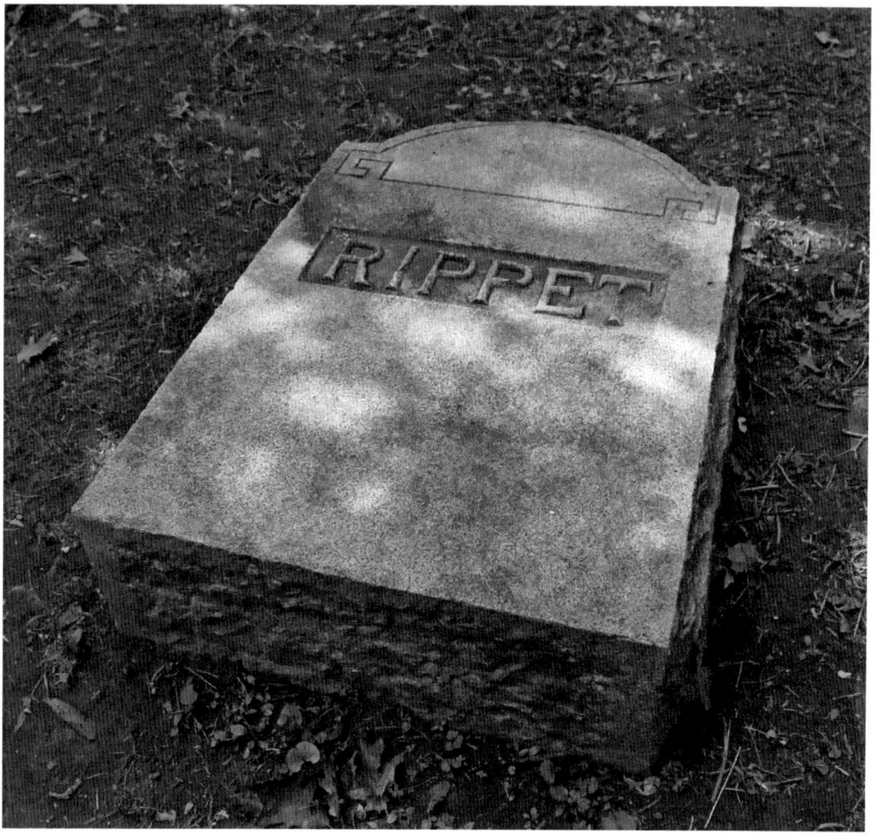

The Rippet family stone has been toppled for generations. The family were dairy farmers, and one member was a Blue Island police officer. *Wendy Moxley Roe.*

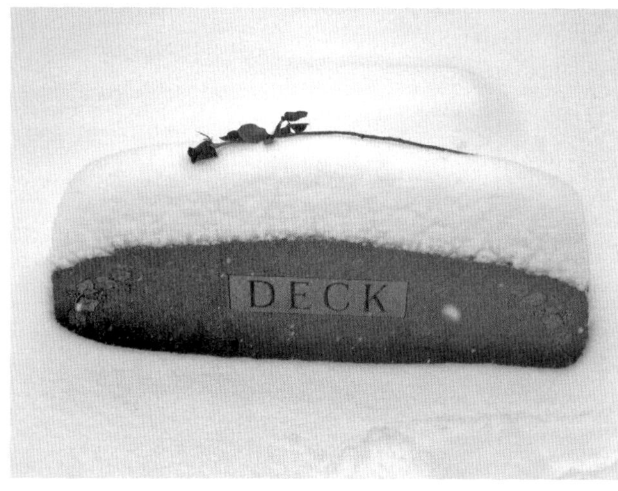

Jennie Deck and her husband, Joseph Niklas, were killed together in a railroad-crossing accident. They are interred here with Jennie's parents, Jacob and Mary, and her brother Bernard. *Wendy Moxley Roe.*

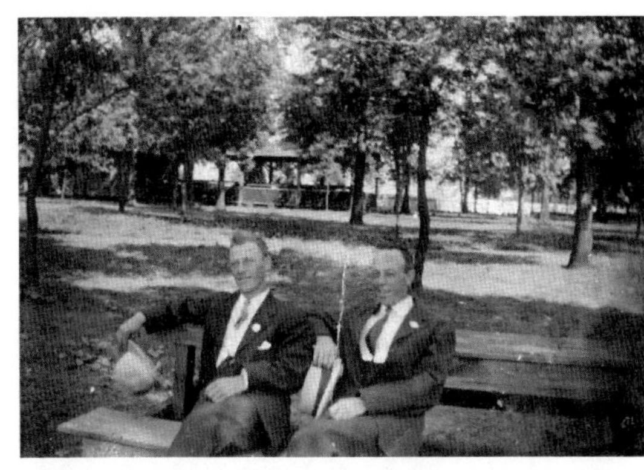

Bernard "Bernie" Deck, interred at Bachelors Grove, visits with one of the Schmidt family descendants in the 1930s. *The Schmidt family.*

during the World's Fair of 1893, after the death of her husband. Returning to England and remarrying, she again visited Bremen Township after her second husband's death. During that visit, in 1906, Edna became too ill to return home. She passed away and was interred here. Her son Albert lived over the creek, likely in the house whose foundation may still be seen there today. Her mother was originally interred here but was moved to the family's plot in town, where Albert and her other children are also interred. This woman, then, with two fruitful marriages and seventeen children, is alone at Bachelors Grove, an ocean away from home.

The last known burial at Bachelors Grove was in this quadrant: at the Shields family lot. The Shields stone is one of the largest still remaining at Bachelors Grove, though it toppled long ago. The burial was of the ashes of Robert Shields in 1989, when mortician Clay Krueger made the trek to the cemetery with a family friend of the deceased to inter the cremains. The photo on the following page shows the state of the family marker the day of the burial in 1989.

The northwest quadrant of the cemetery houses two important sites for visitors: the Fulton stone and the entrance to the quarry pond. Also here is some of the only coping (stone fencing) found in the cemetery today, marking more mysterious graves. Original cemetery plat notations assign these to Louis and Johanna Buch, but while there was a couple with these names living nearby, they farmed in Palos and are buried in Worth. No burial records have been found for this lot, though a 1935 newspaper article describes a headstone or headstones indicating that the Buchs are, indeed, interred here. A map of the cemetery showing transfers of the lots shows an "L. Brock" as the original owner, with the Buchs listed beneath. I found a pioneer named John Bock (an Americanized version of "Buch") on the 1880s census, living in Bremen Township with his son Louis. They were

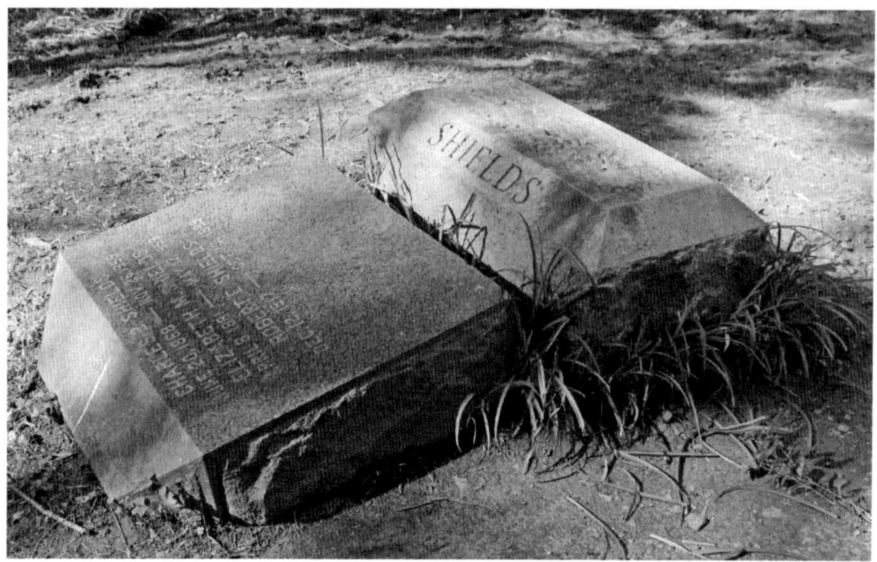

The marker over the Shields family lot was toppled years ago, but it still marks the many graves of this strong local family. The very last known burial at Bachelors Grove took place here when the ashes of Robert Shields were interred in October 1989. *Wendy Moxley Roe.*

both farmers and widowers (Louis was only forty at the time). It is almost certainly this Louis Bock who is interred here, along with his wife. It's also almost certain that John Bock was also interred here, perhaps with his own wife. If the elder Bocks ever had headstones, they were gone by 1935.

The most famous tombstone at Bachelors Grove Cemetery is also the largest of the few still standing. The "Fulton Stone" has stood through generations of varying tranquility and turmoil, not unlike the dynamic family interred below. The Fulton family stone stands on an increasingly unstable base where the path splits, one artery leading into the cemetery's northwest quadrant and the other down to the old quarry beyond the northern fence.

The Fultons would emerge as one of the most important and influential families of the Bachelors Grove and Tinley Park communities. An extensive network of parents, siblings, children and grandchildren, the Fulton line still thrives in Tinley Park and even became world famous through marriage into the Bettenhausen family of racing fame. One of the children of John Fulton Sr., John Fulton Jr., was interred at Bachelors Grove after his death in 1922. The dates on the stone (see page 86) silently tell some of the tragic family story of the Fultons. Though infant and child mortality was high at the time they lived, John and his wife, Hulda Turney Fulton, experienced more than

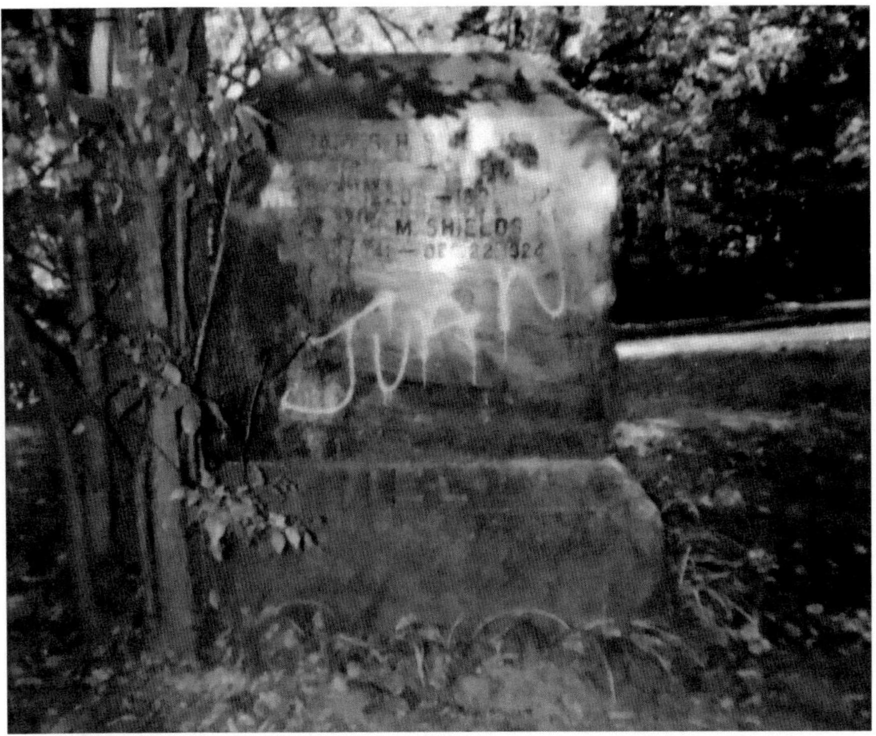

The Shields monument as it looked on the day of the burial of the ashes of Robert Shields, the last known interment at the Grove. *Clay Krueger, Krueger Funeral Home, Blue Island.*

their share, losing son Johnnie B. at the age of ten and an older son, Frank, at thirty-two. John's brother Robert Fulton took his own life by throwing himself in front of a train at the age of thirty-one. Daughter Luella Fulton was struck by a hit-and-run driver in January 1937 while walking on Oak Park Avenue (Batchelor Grove Road) at the age of sixty-five. Abandoned in a ditch, her cries were finally heard by a passerby, but Luella died of internal injuries in a nearby hospital.

Today, thousands of visitors each year make the ritualistic visit to the Fulton stone, many bringing toys, candy, stuffed animals and flowers to place at the attendant stone reading "Infant Daughter," which marks the grave of little Marci May Fulton, daughter of John and Hulda's son Bert Fulton and his wife, Katherine Vogt. She was formerly known as "Marcia" due to public records; however, family records verify that her name was actually Marci. The Vogt family was one of the most important families in Bremen Township, but according to local historians, the Fultons and Vogts

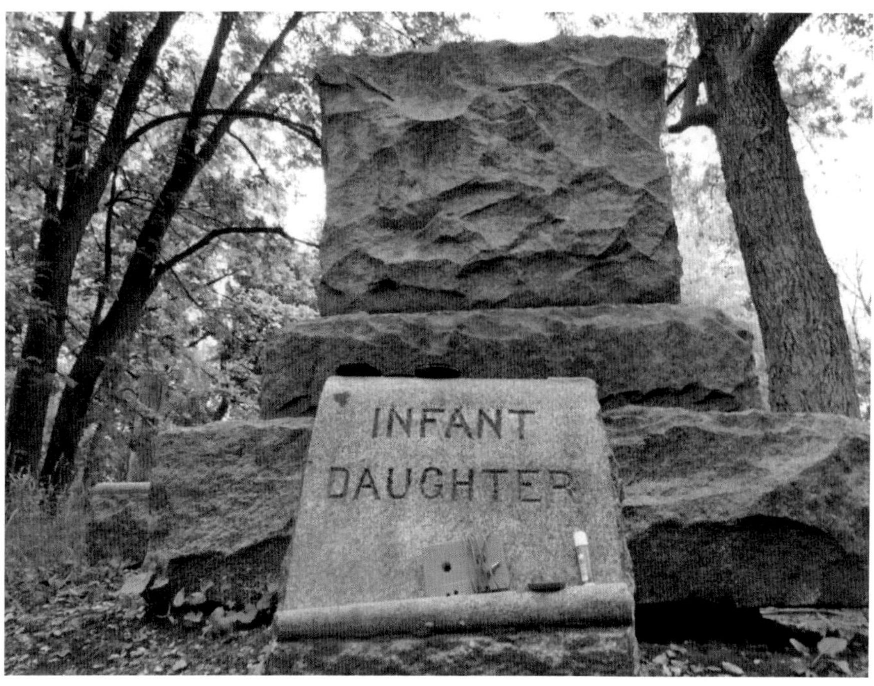

Above: The "Fulton Stone" is the largest stone still standing at Bachelors Grove. It marks the graves of numerous family members, including John Fulton Jr. and Hulda Turney Fulton, robust pioneers whose family line still thrives in the area today. *Wendy Moxley Roe.*

Below: The grave of little Marci May Fulton is marked by a headstone reading "Infant Daughter." The stone has become a year-round shrine; visitors leave everything from candy and coins to toys, hair ornaments and seashells as tokens of affection. *Author's collection.*

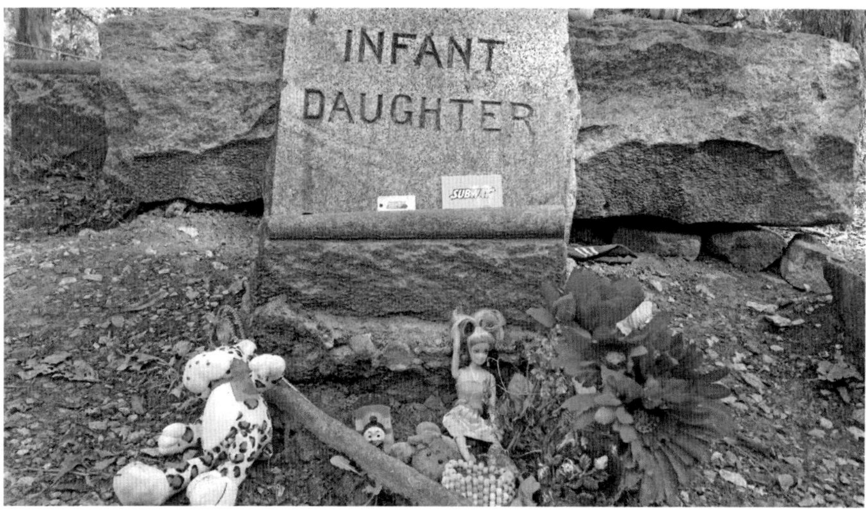

did not get along very well at the time, and the Vogts did not approve of their daughter's marriage to Bert. Marrying anyway, the two gave birth to a daughter, who perished. Though the Vogts owned a large mausoleum, which may still be seen today, in Tinley Park's Zion Lutheran Cemetery, the child was buried at the Fulton lot at Bachelors Grove. Years later, after her own death, Katherine was interred in town, far from her infant child.

The stone of little Emma Fulton, age eleven days, was also placed here upon her death and burial at the lot and then was stolen from Bachelors Grove but recovered. It is today in the care of the Tinley Park Historical Society. The stone, in excellent condition due to its sheltered location, reads:

God's lovely bud, so young and fair.

As time moved on, later Fultons began to choose burial in town, at Zion Lutheran Cemetery, where numerous children and grandchildren are interred. A cenotaph or memorial stone placed in Tinley Park's Zion Lutheran Cemetery near other Fulton family members commemorates the Fultons buried at Bachelors Grove, though no bodies have been moved.

Also in this quadrant is the lot of the John Hamilton family. The stone that resides here today was stolen at an undetermined time in the past but recovered in a recent summer, when Bachelors Grove advocate Peter Crapia was contacted by a Joliet man who had found it in his backyard years before but had no idea where it belonged. When he discovered that it belonged at the Grove, he contacted Crapia, who returned it to its proper location on the cemetery grounds. William Hamilton, John's father, was one of the first "bachelors" to settle here. He traveled to New York City from County Down, Ireland, around 1830. He and Dexter Gilson—another original settler of Bachelors Grove—boarded together in a cabin before starting their own families. Gilson hosted one of the area's first schools on his homestead nearby.

Also in the northwest quadrant is the lot of the Warren family. Ezra Snow Warren and his wife, Susan Lamsen, went west from Vermont in the 1840s, having been given a wagon, a team of oxen and $500 in gold by their fathers as wedding gifts. Family tradition holds that Susan was a cousin of President Martin Van Buren. Ezra and Susan had two sons who fought in the American Civil War. Stephen was enlisted for only three months, from July to October 1862. Richard was captured at the Battle of Ware Bottom Church in Virginia in June 1864. He was incarcerated at Andersonville Prison (Camp Sumter) and was mustered out in December 1865 in Norfolk,

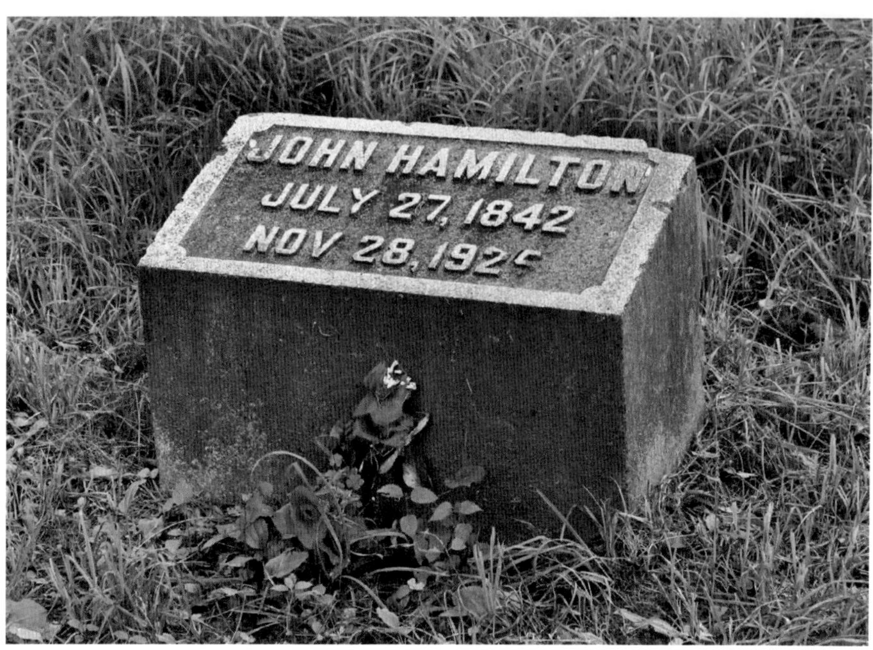

Above: This headstone of John Hamilton was recently recovered from the home of a Joliet man who found it in his home when he purchased it years ago. In recent years, he discovered it belonged in Bachelors Grove and contacted cemetery advocate Peter Crapia, who rescued and returned it to its rightful place. Numerous missing stones are reported to still exist in private homes in the area. They were stolen by young people decades ago, and present tenants either don't know where the stones belong or are afraid to return them, fearing prosecution. I've spoken to people who keep them in their backyards, decorated with lovingly tended flowers; those who display them in their homes and light candles for the deceased; and those who simply keep them in the basement or garage, not knowing what to do with them. *Wendy Moxley Roe.*

Opposite: Ezra Stone Warren and his wife, Susan Lamsen, were given a team of oxen and $500 in gold when they went west in the earliest days of settlement. They are interred at Bachelors Grove with their sons Stephen and Richard, both Civil War soldiers. *Wendy Moxley Roe.*

Virginia. Richard went on to marry Charlotte Hatch. They had a daughter, also Charlotte, in 1868. Family stories say he was "never the same" after the war. He died of tuberculosis at the age of thirty.

The final quadrant is the southwest sector. Here lies the Newman family, near the western fence. Dora (Flassig) Newman was born in 1870 to Frank and Dora Flassig, a large Bachelors Grove family. Daniel Newman, Dora's husband, was the son of John and Rosanna (Turney) Newman. Rosanna was the sister of Hulda (Turney) Fulton, buried at the large

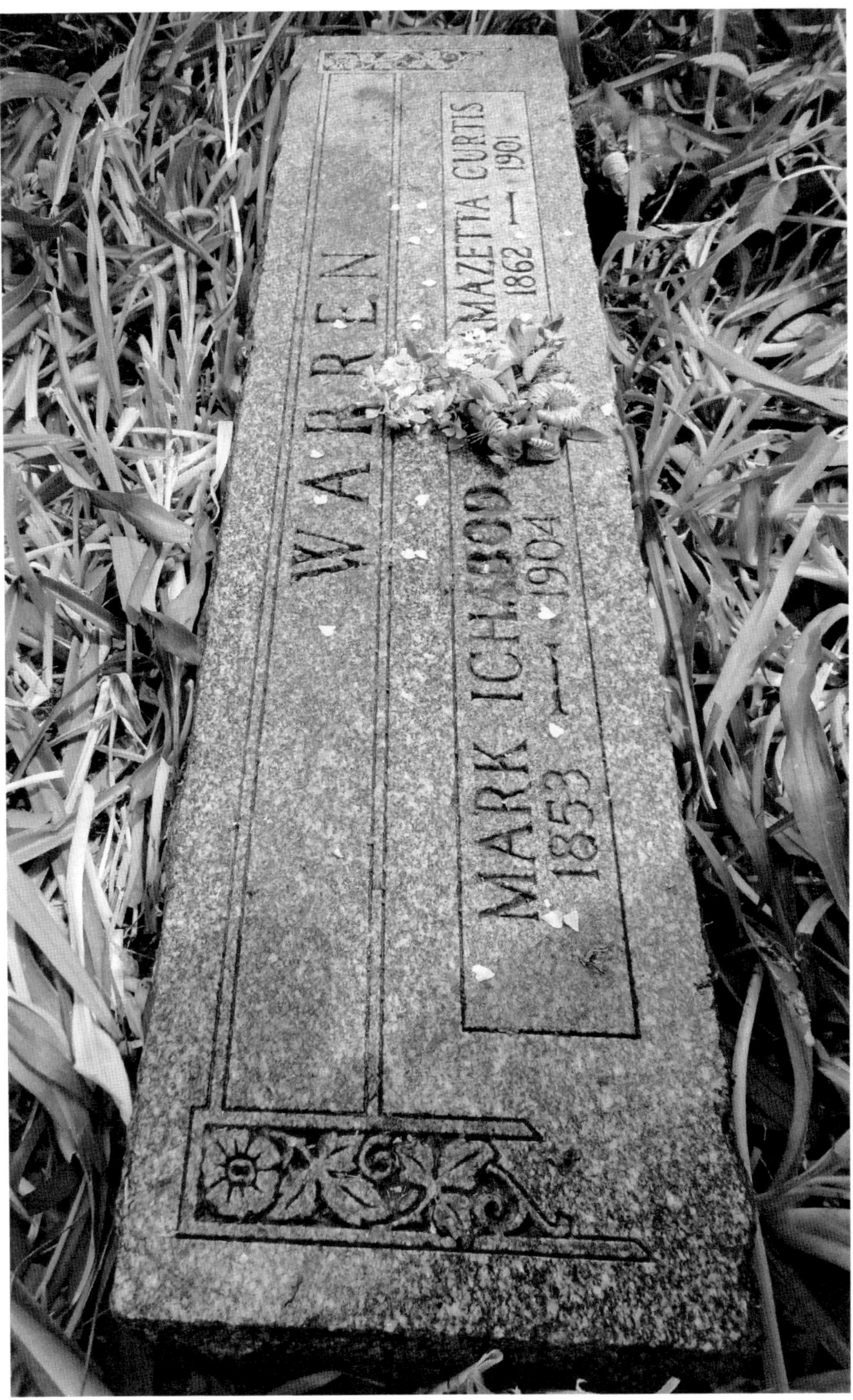
WARREN
MAZETTIA CURTIS
1862 — 1901
MARK
1853 — 1904

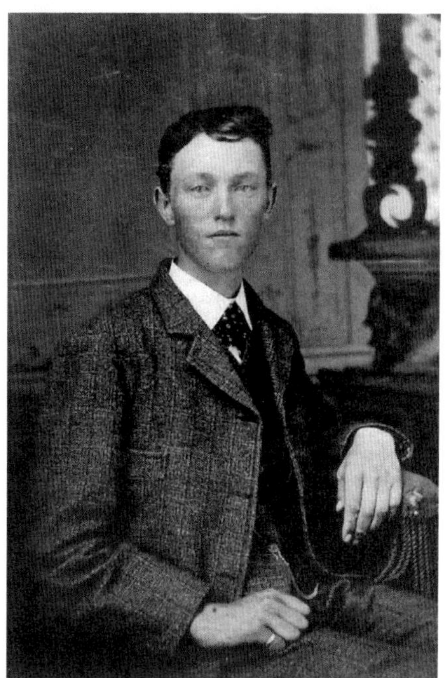

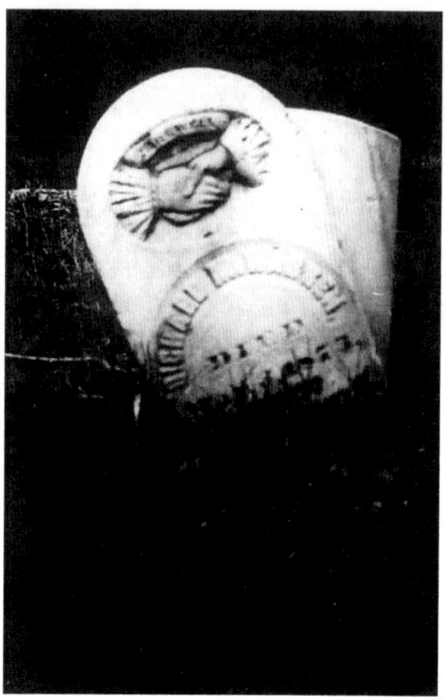

Left: Richard Warren was incarcerated at Andersonville prison after his capture at the Battle of Ware Bottom Church during the American Civil War. He died of tuberculosis at the age of thirty in 1875. *The Warren family.*

Right: This is one of three Warren family headstones, which were stolen sometime after 1951, when this photograph was taken at the cemetery by a family member. *The Warren family.*

Fulton stone at Bachelors Grove. In the very corner of this quadrant is the last known lot at Bachelors Grove. Unmarked, it holds members of the Newman/Stratzenberg (or Sturtzenberg) families, including Hattie Theresa Stratzenberg Adams and her infant children, as well as another Hattie (Therese) Stratzenberg—likely a niece—whose mother and father are unknown at this time.

Also here, next to a tree stump, is the lot of James Fullerton, a Blue Island farmer born in Scotland. He met his wife, Sarah Chapman, in England in the 1860s, and the two immigrated to Illinois, where James farmed until his death. They are interred here together.

Across the path from the couple is the famed "checkered stone" or "quilted stone": the scene where the "Madonna of Bachelor Grove" photo was taken in 1991. This is believed to be the base stone of a now-vanished monument to members of the Rick family.

Right: The most internationally famous stone at Bachelors Grove is doubtless this "checkered" or "quilted" stone base, believed to mark the graves of Rick family members. In 1991, Judy Huff-Felz took one of the most celebrated and controversial "spirt photographs" of all time, showing a diaphanous woman in white sitting on this stone. *Wendy Moxley Roe.*

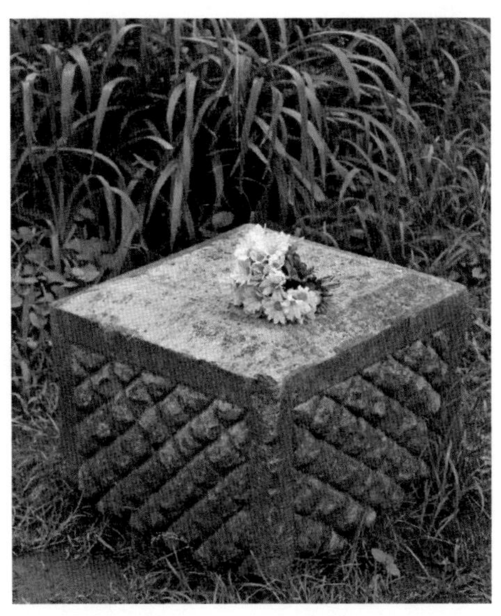

Below: The Hageman family marker is sometimes found in three pieces and sometimes "put back together" by well-meaning visitors. Though such attempts are generous and kind, preservationists warn that they lead to incremental damage and, probably eventually, the breaking of the individual pieces. A proper job by skilled restorationists would include the use of metal rods and improved mortar to permanently bond such separated monument pieces together. *Wendy Moxley Roe.*

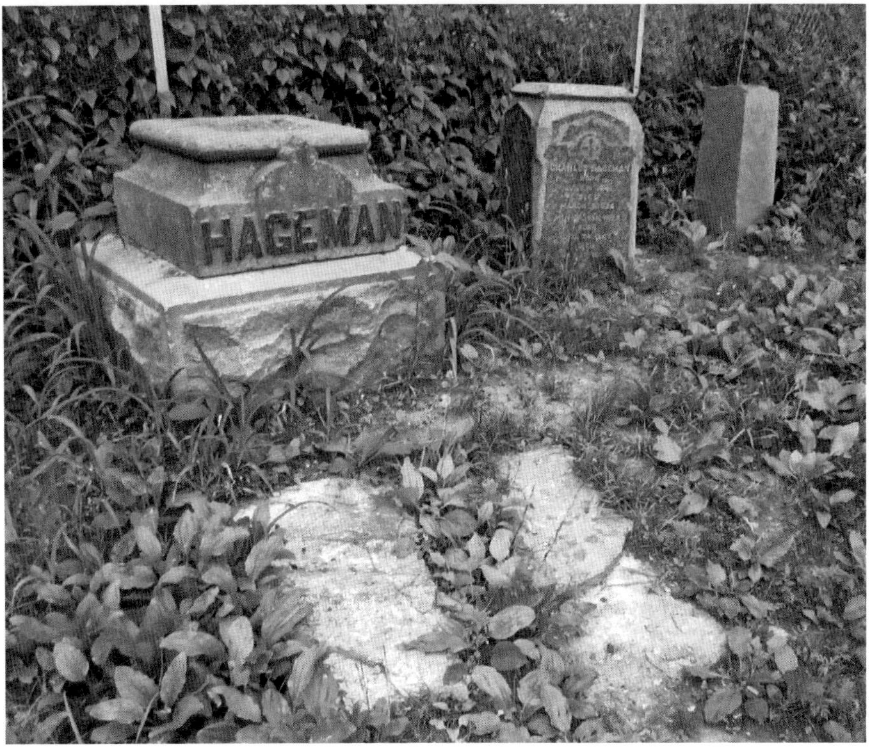

At the cemetery entrance in this quadrant is the lot of the Hageman and Cool families, some of the earliest settlers in Bremen Township, though the Cools were reinterred elsewhere. Jane Nobles Cool was the daughter of William Nobles, the first known burial here.

Many other individuals remain here, both under these stones and in unmarked graves. The process of learning about them all is an ongoing one. These have been shared to give readers and visitors a general idea of the community whose burial ground this was—and is—and a look into the lives of courage and tragedy they endured.

Part II
The Haunting of Bachelors Grove

One night, just before Halloween during my sophomore year at college, I and several others were gathered in a friend's room in the underclassmen's dormitory. Matt, a chemistry major with a personality and voice reminiscent of comedian Jim Carrey, was telling ghost stories. The lights in the room were off, and he held a lit Zippo lighter under his face as he told tales of his native Oak Lawn, one of many villages that make up Chicago's south suburbs, and of the richly storied surrounding towns. It was on this night that I first heard of "Monk's Castle," the limestone church of St. James at Sag Bridge and its haunted burial ground; it was the first time I heard of the phantom hearse of Archer Woods, a black carriage driven by a team of mad horses. And it was the first time I heard of Bachelors Grove.

Matt told what I would come to discover is a classic tale of what he and others called "The Grove." One night in high school, he and some friends had driven to Bachelors Grove to hike through the woods to the cemetery, which was a popular place for drinking, "making out" and general teenaged shenanigans.

The night was cold. Fall had come early, and the kids shuddered as they sat on crumbling tombstones, talking and sharing the cans of beer they had carried in their coat pockets. After some time, an eerie feeling came over them, as if they were being watched. Suddenly, a flashing blue light appeared through the trees. Expecting that the local police had discovered them in the preserve—off-limits after sundown—the three friends bolted down the path

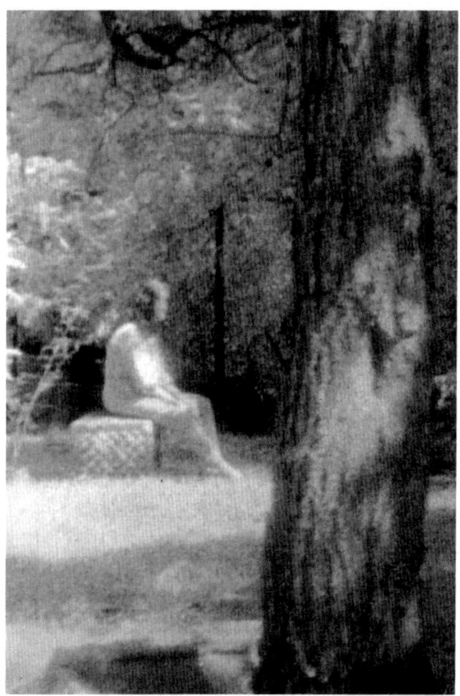

Judy Huff-Felz took this famous photograph during an investigation by the Ghost Research Society in August 1991. It has been examined by photographic experts and camera manufacturers, including Kodak, and declared "authentic." This means that whatever appears in the photograph was not the result of camera or film issues or of fraudulent manipulation of these. The camera, then, captured what it saw. *Judy Huff-Felz.*

toward the adjacent creek, as the bridge that once spanned it was long gone: they could easily cross it on foot and find freedom in the woods beyond—and the path through to Ridgeland Avenue.

But as the young men sprinted across the creek bed, they were stunned to find that the flashing light had also crossed the creek bed—easily six feet below the road and along a path too narrow for a car—and was pursuing them into the forest. This was no police car. This was one of the many mysterious lights that had been reported at the Grove for at least thirty years.

Matt told us other stories of the Grove. The story of the Madonna in white who traversed the woods endlessly, in search of her baby. The story of the "magic house" that appeared and disappeared along the path to the cemetery. The story of the black cars and phantom dogs that silently stalked trespassers on the fabled cemetery grounds. With each word, I fell deeper under the spell that many well know.

As so many have come to find, Bachelors Grove had me at hello.

Truly, I could not get Bachelors Grove out of my head after that night. But though I had access to millions of books through our college interlibrary loan system, references to this compelling place in this pre-Internet world were scarce at best. I found a clipping of a yellowed *Chicago Tribune* article that interviewed Chicago's "original ghost hunter," the late Richard Crowe, who talked about a "dream house" that would appear and disappear in the woods around the cemetery. I found the wonderful book *Psychic City: Chicago: Doorway to Another Dimension* by the great Brad Steiger and the classic *Haunted*

Heartland by Beth Scott and Michael Norman. But that was all. As for going to the source? Without a car, and before suburban bus systems, Bachelors Grove might as well have been on the moon.

Amazingly, that same year I met the man who introduced me to the science of parapsychology. Jim Houran was a student in psychology, and the department was allowing him to focus much of his studies on psi, or parapsychological research. It was through our friendship that I became a research assistant in parapsychological fieldwork and came to work on my first investigations into the paranormal. Some of these first investigations were at Bachelors Grove.

The very first of these was part of a series of experiments focused on the Grove: Are more anomalous photographs actually taken there than at other cemeteries? Are visitors predisposed to having anomalous experiences there because of the site's notoriety? Are the electrical and magnetic fields at the site regulated by paranormal factors?

I will never forget my first visit to this place, walking the path through the woods to this lost little burial ground. Just inside the gate, which at the time was padlocked but with a human-size rip down it serving as an entry, in front of the stone marking the Moss family burials, a plastic doll's hand had been stuck in the dirt, a cigarette held between its fingers, as if some long-dead resident was reaching up for an afternoon smoke.

The sight should have chilled me, and certainly I was appalled by this sacrilege. But there was something else, too, that came through.

"Hello!" this token seemed to say. "We're here. We're hanging out on this beautiful day. Come on in and get to know us."

It was a gloriously sunny summer afternoon, and I saw what many still describe upon a first visit: an astoundingly magical place. I saw that the play of light in the cemetery is unusual and could certainly trick the eye and cause rampant simulacra to be created. Everywhere I looked, it seemed, there was a face on a tombstone, a pair of eyes in the bark of a tree, a child stepping through the grass. Most of all, I was overwhelmed by the feeling of peace that many visitors experience, and there was no way to reconcile my emotional response with the dreadful reputation of this site.

This was my first experience of the "moods" of Bachelors Grove that frequent visitors know very well. Like any living, breathing entity, the Grove is sometimes happy—and sometimes decidedly not. It sometimes shows itself and wants to play and sometimes pulls the covers over its head until you leave. Sometimes, too, Bachelors Grove *makes* you leave.

During those first visits, nothing out of the ordinary happened to back up the extraordinary international fame of the site, though our photography experiments did suggest that more blacked-out or whited-out photographs did, in fact, seem to be produced there. The results of those experiments were eventually published in the *Journal of Perceptual and Motor Skills*, and to my knowledge, this remains some of the only academic research ever published about Bachelors Grove.

By the time of publication, Jim and I had long before graduated and parted ways, he into the world of academic psychology and I into graduate studies in history. But I had not seen the last of Bachelors Grove. Over the next thirty years, I would come to witness the many moods of this complex, elusive place, from kind to cutthroat. Though, thirty years later, I have—realizing its unpredictable power—sworn a hundred times to never go back, I expect I never will stop.

Variously called the "Most Haunted Cemetery in Chicago," the "Most Haunted Place in Chicago" and even the "Most Haunted Cemetery on Earth," Bachelors Grove has been both a mecca for ghost hunters and a thorn in the side of the county for generations. For investigators like me, it's become a second home from which we can't long stay away.

7
LEGENDS OF BACHELORS GROVE

Despite the many witnessed phenomena at the place, Bachelors Grove is probably most famous for the grim legends that have been localized here for generations, as they have in places like this around the world. For Bachelors Grove is the classic setting for tales of horror: the lovers' lane outside a crumbling cemetery, down an abandoned road through the woods. It's an inspiring spot for ghost stories, and local teens and young people have met the challenge for nearly a century. These "urban legends," at Bachelors Grove and elsewhere, have often been shrugged off by major folklorists like Jan Harold Brunvand as nothing but tall tales, but other folklorists such as Michael Wilson are realizing that there are almost always grains of truth in these tales—and that these tales are periodically recharged by local true events that line up nicely with the age-old stories. I have found many elements of Bachelors Grove's famous horror myths in true events that have happened at the Grove or in neighboring areas, but it is these, the Grove's notorious legends, that have secretly held the clues for so long and that provided these when I went in search of what really happened.

THE BOYFRIEND'S DEATH

One of the most famous legends of Bachelors Grove has been a popular urban legend around the United States and the United Kingdom since at least the 1940s. Known typically as "The Boyfriend's Death," the story tells of a teen couple who parks in a "lovers' lane" in the woods. When the boy becomes too passionate, the girl asks to be taken home, but the car won't start. After several tries, the boy leaves the girl to walk to the road and flag down help. After he departs, the wind stirs up as a storm comes in. The trees are creaking and bending in the wind, and the girl hears the branches scraping the top of the car. She's uneasy but stays put until she gratefully sees flashing blue lights coming down the road. When the girl gets out of the car, she's surprised to see that her boyfriend is not with the police officers in the car. They say to her, "Just walk toward us and don't turn around." Of course, the girl turns around, and when she does she sees her boyfriend hanging upside down over their car, his throat slit from ear to ear and his fingernails scraping the top of the car.

This story has been "localized" in many parts of the United States and United Kingdom for generations, meaning that local young people will claim that this universal tale "really happened" in their own town or area. For generations, too, folklorists dismissed these stories as just stories—urban legends meant as warning lessons to young people. But as we shall see, the truth may be truer than we want to believe. Indeed, numerous locals, including police officers, have claimed that this incident actually happened at Bachelors Grove, some testifying that they even saw the police report and the crime scene photos, of which more later.

THE HOOK

Another immensely popular tale at Bachelors Grove is that of "The Hook" or "The Hooked Maniac." In this tale, another couple is parked along a dark forest road one night, kissing, the radio playing softly. Suddenly, the music is interrupted by an emergency announcement: a killer has escaped the nearby asylum and is on the loose in the area. He is identifiable by a hook he wears in place of a missing hand. The girl is terrified and begs to be taken home immediately. The young man grudgingly obliges, but when they arrive at her house and he goes around to open her door, the young man finds a rusted hook swinging from the door handle: the killer had been ready to open the girl's car door as he pulled out of the woods. Interestingly, there is a "one-armed sniper" or "one-armed caretaker" who has been tied to Bachelors Grove, often as part of a phantom caretaker legend. Could a local resident have lost a hand in a farming or factory accident and worn one of the primitive, hook-like prosthetics of the day? Or perhaps the man was a World War I or even Civil War veteran, of which there were many living in Bremen Township during the purging of the settlers from their land? Did this settler perhaps confront young couples who were parking in the "lovers' lane" or in the cemetery, startling them with his unusual appearance? With the widespread circulation of the story of "The Hook" in the 1930s and '40s, it would not be surprising if local teenagers transformed an unfortunate and well-meaning neighbor into a "Hooked Maniac."

THE CARETAKER

For generations, most people held a deeply skewed idea of what Bachelors Grove was and is. The general thought was that this had always been natural forest, that the cemetery had been established in this strangely isolated area and that there were no property records for any houses or other buildings in its vicinity. These beliefs helped encourage the creation or spread of stories that grew up around the "mysterious" house foundations in the woods, buoyed by sightings of a ghost house, which seem to have begun in the 1960s. As we will see, there may be at least some true events that led to one of the Grove's most widespread tales: the story of "The Caretaker."

According to the legend, there was once an official caretaker of Bachelors Grove Cemetery, and he and his family lived in a modest house in the woods nearby. All was well until, one night, voices from the cemetery told him to take an axe and kill his family. As if transfixed, he completed the gruesome deed. At its completion, he snapped out of his trance and realized what he had done and, in horror, hanged himself in a tree outside the cemetery gates. When the townspeople discovered what he had done, they burned down the house and torched the property records, hoping to eradicate all trace and memory of what had happened.

As we will see, real caretakers did exist in the history of the Grove, as did elements of all of these tales of horror. Sure, the stories grew. But just how much? At Bachelors Grove, are the true stories, in fact, at least as troubling as the legends they left behind?

8
GRAINS OF TRUTH

As with all such stories, the Bachelors Grove legends began when something went terribly wrong. Some of these unfortunate incidents have been uncovered, while some remain hidden even to rigorous researchers like me.

In all of the Cook County forest preserves, from time to time, accidents happen. Bachelors Grove has been no different. Until the time of the turnpike's closing, a bridge spanned the tributary of Tinley Creek (originally called Bachelors Grove Creek) that flows through the preserve and past the cemetery. Travelers by wagon or car along the turnpike had to cross this bridge in order to clear the creek. But when the bridge was removed, only foot traffic could still traverse the creek, and only then when the water was not too high to cross it. In 1951, the recent removal of the bridge led to a tragic accident when a carload of travelers took the old turnpike road as a shortcut, unaware that the bridge had been removed. The water was about six feet deep at the time, and one of the passengers perished. This was not the only car to end up in the creek, apparently, as local resident Bill Swinford in 2013 found the fuel pump from a Model A Ford in the creek near the quarry pond, much too heavy to have been washed up- or downstream from elsewhere.

One researcher reported hearing from a local resident that, while the turnpike road was still open, a man was riding with his head out of the car window while traveling at a clip and had his head severed by a low-hanging tree branch. The friend told of another decapitation, in which an anonymous perpetrator strung wires between trees and then chased out visitors, causing one to have his head sliced off by a taut wire that caught him at just the right—or wrong—spot.

As previously mentioned, Clarence Fulton, a prominent member of the community and the last cemetery trustee, went on record about the drownings of children that occurred in the quarry pond when he was a child growing up in the area, presumably by those unaware of the dangers of quarry swimming when this was the area fishing and swimming hole.

These woods are no stranger to purposeful death, either, and documented stories of murder and suicide exist here as well, dating much further back than anyone might imagine.

A well-known and documented story of murder here was a 1966 incident in which a local man hunting mushrooms discovered the slain body of Audry Ellis in the woods near Ridgeland Avenue and 145th Street. The girl, wearing only a gold bracelet and a shamrock necklace, was discovered to have been from Gary, Indiana, and had been on her way to a job interview. She is one of three young women found murdered in the forest preserves of Cook County that year, and her murder remains unsolved.

Less well known, though much more recent, was a strange incident that occurred in 1989, in which a local unemployed truck driver, Martin Myers, while awaiting trial for first-degree murder, was found dead outside the entrance to Bachelors Grove Cemetery. He had been shot in the head by his girlfriend, who had lured Myers to the cemetery to kill him after he beat her and held a gun to her head. Earlier that year, Myers had hit an associate head-on with his pickup truck and killed him because he had vied for the attentions of this same woman. Myers's own murder occurred days before he was to stand trial for the deed.

These incidents have been easily found by rudimentary searches through publications archives, but there are incidents concerning Bachelors Grove that have been whispered about for generations but that have not yielded themselves to even relentless research.

Folklorist Michael Wilson demonstrates that urban legends, whatever their origin, may be recharged by current events that spark new interest in and local memory of the original stories. When I was first starting out as a young author in the 1990s, making the circuit of local libraries with my lectures, I was frequently astounded by the many firsthand accounts brought forth by audience members of stories about Bachelors Grove I'd assumed were urban legends. Time and again, patrons would remain behind after my speaking to tell me that these stories were, in fact, true.

But while all links to truth have been intriguing, there is one story that has haunted me for nearly two decades: the story that was told to me as true in the autumn of 1997, at one of my very first lectures.

After my talk, I was literally speechless when a man came up to me and said he was intrigued by my telling of "The Boyfriend's Death" legend at Bachelors Grove, because he'd gone to high school with the boy who was killed. In the tale, a local student is supposedly found hanging upside down in a tree outside the cemetery with his throat slit. I did not know what to say, so I stupidly said, "That's just a story!" No, he insisted. The young man had attended the local public high school with him and had his throat slit and his body hung from a tree outside the cemetery entrance. His date, who had been waiting for him in the car, was institutionalized afterward for a time from the shock, he said.

I gave him my number and asked him to please call me so I could interview him and get the details for further research. I never heard from him again.

For the next fifteen years, I asked everyone I met who had grown up in the area if they knew anything about this. When I met a retired policeman or sheriff's deputy, I begged them to comb their memories and ask their colleagues if they knew of any incident like this. But no one did. I spent endless hours running search terms through databases of newspaper articles: "oak forest" and "slain…oak forest"; "woods" and "dead…Midlothian"; "preserve" and "slain." I tried every combination I could think of that might lead to a story I was looking for; that is, if it had really happened. I found nothing.

On Halloween in 2012, I was at Bachelors Grove Cemetery with a number of friends, having a picnic and meeting other visitors, when I met a retired police officer and his wife from the area. Amazingly, he told me that he had been at a neighboring police station the night this incident happened and that he had seen the police report and the crime scene photos. Like the man who had first told me of the incident years before, he also said that the young woman involved had been institutionalized after the incident. This time I got the contact information for the witness, who urged me to contact him and to come over to their home some night, have a campfire and some cocktails and hear the many local tales they knew.

The next day, I sent an e-mail telling the couple what a pleasure it was to talk with them and that I hoped we could soon arrange our storytelling session. To my surprise, the man returned my e-mail with a curt response: he really didn't know much else about the story. There was really nothing else he could tell me. He wished me good luck and signed off. No further response could be coaxed out of him.

Baffled, all I could do was return to my own search. One night, in late 2013, I found what I had been looking for—or so I thought:

The article was entitled "Man Guilty in Killing of Teen Couple" and was dated August 1988.

The story concerned a man named John Ber, a local loner who had been thrown out of his family's home for stealing. Ber had taken up residence in an abandoned farmhouse owned by his father that stood around 181st Street and Laramie Avenue, about four miles from Bachelors Grove. The local teens knew him to be a bit off and generally avoided his company. But one evening a local couple from nearby Country Club Hills was cruising the area and saw Ber on the porch of the old house. Hoping to buy some beer from the older man, they left the car and approached the house. After a few words on the porch, the two went inside as the girl waited. After a few minutes, Ber came out and motioned the girl inside, where she discovered that Ber had stabbed and slit the throat of her friend. Ber then stabbed the girl multiple times. Her body was found later in a car trunk in the area, with help from a passerby who saw blood outside the car.

The following day, some friends of the dead couple set fire to the house in anger. They were exonerated of all charges. Soon after, the Hickory Hills Fire Department finished burning down the house in a firefighting exercise. At trial, Ber offered no rational motive for the killings, claiming that "a huge, red devil" had appeared to him and told him to kill.

In this story we find numerous pieces from the legends of Bachelors Grove: the young man with his throat slit. The girl waiting in the car. The loner living in a house in the woods. A malevolent spirit telling him to kill. And, lastly, the house being burned down by bitter survivors. Could this story be the source of the gruesome legends at Bachelors Grove?

For a while we thought maybe Jon Ber had visited Bachelors Grove and been somehow inspired to kill, as had the caretaker in the old local legend. In 2014, however, researchers Wendy Moxley Roe and Karl K wrote to the incarcerated John Ber, who assured them that he had never been to Bachelors Grove.

Despite the disconnect, the Ber murders may have "refueled" the existing stories at the Grove, which seem to be much older than the 1988 Ber incident, and incorporated aspects of the new incident into the old story. Indeed, both the witnesses I met and the late ghost hunter Richard Crowe all claimed that the incident of the "man hung upside down" really happened, and at Bachelors Grove Cemetery specifically. Along with the witnesses who insisted to me that it happened, Crowe also claimed that he had credible sources who swore it had actually occurred at Bachelors Grove just as the story says: the young man being hanged upside down in a tree just outside the cemetery; the girlfriend waiting in the car. He told Chicago WIND radio host Eddie Schwartz in July 1977 that "hopefully a certain file which is said to exist will come into my hands in the near future." Crowe said a law-enforcement officer had seen the file and told him about it, promising to get him a copy, and that the incident had probably occurred "in the late 1940s...about '48 or '49." However, my witness claimed it was the early 1980s.

Now, one would think that if such an incident really did happen, local residents would remember it a mere twenty years later, but in the case of the John Ber killings, not one person remembered a gruesome incident involving the tragic murders of two local teens, a house being burned down or this notorious local loner—even after I found the newspaper story and tried to jog their memories with names, dates and specifics. As for the fact that there has been no record of this hanging-man story uncovered in any news archives? Keep in mind that it took me more than twenty years to find the articles about John Ber, which had appeared prominently in the *Chicago Tribune*.

If this incident really did happen, and at that period in time, this might help to explain the fact that the vandalism at Bachelors Grove began in the early 1950s, possibly as a result of the intrigue created by the murder. One day, I believe, the case will be brought to light.

What do we know now about hangings at Bachelors Grove? In fact, the Cook County forest preserves are no stranger to suicide, and we will see that there has been at least one suicide attempt at Bachelors Grove in recent years—an attempt that led to a possibly paranormal intervention. Shockingly, however, the earliest known suicide by hanging here dates to 1913.

That year, Christ Abbe, a local farmer, discovered the body of a young woman in a white dress lashed to a neighbor's fence by a cloth tied around her neck. The young woman, Martine Winther, a Danish seamstress who had been living on Chicago's south side, had boarded a Rock Island train, headed for Audubon, Iowa, where her brother resided. Investigators into the death believed she had jumped from the train somewhere in the area and had been wandering around for many hours when she was heard moaning outside a Bachelors Grove farmhouse around one o'clock in the morning. Neighbors said she was claiming that the "Black Hand" organization was after her, and a local farmer directed her to the Oak Forest Infirmary for shelter. Without responding, she turned and ran down the road, disappearing. She never made it to the hospital.

The *Chicago Tribune* reported the story on July 19, 1913:

> *The body of a young woman, possibly 25 years old, was suspended from a cross bar between the fence posts. A strip of cloth of white wash material, evidently torn from a dress, had been drawn around the woman's neck and tied to the post. Her feet touched the ground, and if it were suicide it was necessary for her to lift her body partially from the ground in order to hang herself. Her arms extended stiff against her sides.*

After an investigation initiated by Bremen Township supervisor Samuel Fulton, local medical officials declared that Winther had died by suicide. Her brother Christopher Winther claimed her body and buried her near his home in Iowa.

9
The Witnessed Activity

In all my years of paranormal research and investigation, there is no single place at which I have documented more ostensibly paranormal activity and collected more reports of such than Bachelors Grove. The activity spans literally every type of experience that people have in the realm of the Other Side, from apparitions to physical effects on their bodies to encounters with strange lights and even cryptids. Those recorded here are literally only a fraction of those that I—just one person—have experienced or been told of. The true breadth and scope of the Grove's manifestations must be, I think, unfathomable. I'm offering to readers here a representation of the most prevalent phenomena only: those manifestations for which the Grove is famous. I hope readers will consider these as only a stepping-off point for discovery and nowhere near a complete collection.

The Lights of Bachelors Grove

The unexplained lights of Bachelors Grove are some of the most prolific phenomena experienced here or anywhere. In fact, countless visitors and investigators have photographed or filmed these lights, which are seen as often in the daytime as at night and include blue, white, red, green and yellow versions. Many of the apparitions and other phenomena at Bachelors Grove have been accompanied at times by the appearance of inexplicable lights as well.

My own first paranormal experience at Bachelors Grove was of a mysterious, seemingly intelligent white light that many, many visitors have experienced. It was during one of my first visits there, as a research assistant to my colleague Jim Houran in the late 1980s. During an evening investigation, a white ball of light—no bigger than a tennis ball—appeared off "the Path" in a clump of trees. It moved with incredible speed, darting back and forth or winking off and appearing a split-second later a hundred feet away. More than twenty years later, I was amazed to see that this exact same phenomenon had been filmed by the crew of the television show *Ghost Adventures* during a visit to Chicago in the summer of 2012.

A red light has also been seen by visitors to the cemetery, sometimes described as rocket-like or as a shooting or streaking light, suggesting that this light is not circular or spherical but comet-like, with a tail of some sort. This light has been seen both on the old turnpike path, east and west of the cemetery, as well as in the burying ground itself. Apparently the appearances of this light were at first mistaken for fireworks being shot off, having the appearance of roman candles or other such amusements. But a strange behavior ruled out the prospect; several witnesses were startled to see that, after the initial "shooting" or "streaking" or even a "shower of sparks," the light was still there, but floating or bobbing among the tombstones.

As chronicled in the introduction to this section, the first tale I heard of the Grove was of the most famous of its lights: a blue flashing light that had "chased" my classmate across the creek and into the woods in the early 1980s. Such incidents are prolific in local oral accounts dating back to the early 1960s. Time and again, witnesses describe a "flashing" or "flickering" blue light, ranging in size from a softball to a balloon and larger, which seems intelligent to the point of pursuing them through the cemetery or down the turnpike path into the woods or toward the creek. Some visitors have actually been close enough to "touch" the blue light, most notably a local woman named Denise Travis, who famously told ghost hunter Richard Crowe that she had passed a hand through the light, feeling no difference in temperature or other strange sensations. One of the first anomalous photographs I took at the cemetery (circa 1988) showed an arc of blue light partially eclipsing the frame of the image.

A smattering of locals remembers a chilling but as yet unsubstantiated incident that reportedly occurred in 1963, the first year I have been able to verify a sighting of the blue light. According to the tale, three local boys had gone into the woods surrounding the cemetery and went missing for several weeks. When they finally wandered out of the woods, unharmed, they could not remember anything about the weeks during which they had vanished except that they had followed a mysterious blue light.

That year would bring other brushes with the blue light, including an incident that occurred around Halloween, when a group of five young men visiting the cemetery all witnessed the light in unison, in the wee hours of the morning. They had gathered on the old overlook next to the quarry pond—now gone—when they saw a blue light moving on the water toward them. In fear, the men retreated to their cars and claimed to have been chased by the light down the new turnpike road (143rd Street) as they fled.

Also in that year, a couple who had "parked" on the south side of the cemetery along the old turnpike road claims to have seen a blue light, the size of a basketball, meander up the path from the creek area, turn sharply into the cemetery gates and head out past the Fulton stone toward the quarry pond.

Like the stories of the magic house, many witnesses of the blue light have claimed that the light shrinks or moves farther away as it is approached or even tries to lead them into confusion. This was the case for three young women who tried to follow the light across the creek in the summer of 1989, only to find themselves turned around and quite lost when the light suddenly "switched off" like a light bulb.

Though many years passed after my first encounters with the lights of Bachelors Grove, the lights would visit me again, and this time with malice. In late June 2012, I was in the woods at night with a steward of the cemetery and experienced one of the most extraordinary visual manifestations I have ever seen. It was an exceptionally hot, humid night, and as we walked through the woods toward the cemetery, there was an increasing sense of the impression that visitors here often describe as "enchanted" or "magical." I don't know where we were when we saw this. At first I thought we must be overlooking the quarry, as there seemed to be a large expanse of emptiness before us, but I realize now that this could not have been the case, as we walked for a good ten minutes more before arriving at the cemetery.

It is still difficult for me to describe what I saw, but it was a light show of sorts, consisting of thousands of tiny blinking or flashing lights that mimicked flashbulbs going off. The only thing I can compare it to is the image of dozens of paparazzi cameras going off, one after another, at a celebrity gala. I was absolutely mesmerized by this experience, and when I say it seemed to be happening with an intelligence behind it, other experiencers will understand that. It was as if it was happening *for us.*

That experience threw my perceptions off, perhaps also on purpose, for I felt incredibly welcome in our explorations, as if some unseen host were very happy to find us there. We continued to the cemetery and spent about an hour quietly recording in the cemetery for EVP and chatting about the history of the site. Then, at about 10:30 p.m., we left to make our way back to our cars.

It was a very long time before I realized my associate and I had gotten lost. We walked for many long minutes through the brambles and fallen trees that were everywhere. I was wearing a sundress, as I had not expected to walk in the woods, and my legs were slashed repeatedly by various thorns and brush. It was dark with no moon, and we had no flashlight. We both had the idea to use the GPS applications on our cell phones to find which way we were headed, but they had both lost their signals. The possibility of this happening had never crossed my mind. As a fifteen-year veteran researcher of the place, my colleague had personally marked and mapped all the trails through the woods and estimated that he'd visited these woods some two thousand times or more. We could have been no more than two blocks from a suburban road, from houses and businesses. We continued to walk, and my phone drained of power and died. My colleague used the flashlight application on his phone to help us find our footing, but we could see that the light was becoming weaker.

After some time, we began to see a faint light up ahead and thought we had finally neared a road or a subdivision that surrounded the preserve. We could see lights of houses and even see and hear cars passing on the road and, gratefully and with much relief, walked toward them. But the lights seemed to get farther away as we walked, and I thought we must be somehow walking at a diagonal, even though that really made no sense. After some walking, the lights actually disappeared, and it was as if someone had switched off a television: where one moment there were images and sounds, the next moment we were in a vacuum.

This experience repeated over and over, every fifteen or twenty minutes, and it was then that a chilling realization came over us: this was happening on purpose. Something was manipulating the environment to trick us, to tire us and confuse us. With no way to call anyone or find a way out, and thinking of my little girls at home with the babysitter, having no idea where I was, I began to experience a tremendous feeling of panic and despair.

Four and a half hours after we went into the woods, we found our way out through the "back door" entrance that runs along 143rd Street at Central. We were so far away from where we thought we were, and there was really no way we could have been so lost in such a small area for such a long time. I have never forgotten the feeling of that experience, and I have never ventured into those woods again, night or day, off the path. Of course, I was alarmed and amazed to discover, a few years later, the alleged incident in the early 1960s in which a group of boys were lost in the woods at Bachelors Grove for several *weeks* and, when found, unharmed, could not remember anything that had happened except for seeing mysterious lights that had "led them into the woods."

Just what the Bachelors Grove lights are has been a much-discussed subject, as has the subject of ghost lights in general. Medieval observers called such lights "will-o'-the-wisps" or *ignis fatuus*. This term, Latin for "foolish fire," refers to the belief that these lights lured travelers over marshes and swamps at night, away from the road, sometimes to their demise, not unlike some of the Bachelors Grove lights. Interestingly, at the Grove, numerous witnesses to these lights have claimed that the lights "transfixed" or "hypnotized" them, leading them off the main path and into the woods or the high creek, causing them to become lost or even nearly drown; or that the lights had appeared above the quarry pond, similarly "leading" them to a dangerous place.

Ancient folk beliefs claimed these lights were elementals or fairies, and the term "jack-o'-lantern" has its origins in the ghost light phenomenon. According to an ancient story, a man named Jack, too bad for Heaven but turned away by the Devil, stole a piece of coal from Hell's furnace on his way out, which he used as a lantern to light his way, eternally, through the world of the living. Hence, ghost lights seen in cemeteries in particular were called "ghost candles" or "ghost lanterns." Followers of the manifestations of Bachelors Grove will find this fascinating, as a "lantern man" or "candle man" has often been seen at the cemetery entrance, where many of the famed lights also make an appearance. Of this, more later.

Sometimes in folklore, ghost lights are believed to be the spirits of unbaptized or stillborn children, flitting between Heaven and Hell. With the many tragic burials of babies and children at Bachelors Grove, it would not be difficult to connect this bit of folklore to the sightings at the Grove. One paranormal investigator, a medium named David Wismer, claims that a baby was thrown down a well—though now filled in—on the property across the creek on the old turnpike road. Numerous witnesses have seen various lights coming from this direction or headed toward it.

An obscure legend of Bachelors Grove tells of a treasure buried in the quarry pond or under the forest floor. This is compelling, as Irish and other

European folk traditions believed that a ghost light indicated treasure under the ground or water where it appeared. Fascinatingly, rumors have been told at Bachelors Grove of underground tunnels in the woods or of sunken loot under the surface of the pond—perhaps even suitcases full of bootlegging cash in the sunken cars of gangsters.

In Scottish folklore, ghost lights often appeared over lochs or cemetery roads. Once again, this is quite interesting in view of the appearance of the Bachelors Grove lights over the quarry pond and the old turnpike road—the path traveled for generations by funeral corteges to the cemetery gates.

Of course, numerous modern researchers have attempted to explain the natural origins of these lights. The first known serious research into *ignis fatuus* was by the physicist Alessandro Volta, who discovered methane gas. Working in the eighteenth century, Volta wondered if ghost lights might be caused by natural electricity interacting with swamp gases or the gases given off by decomposing bodies. Though several prominent peers supported his hypothesis, Volta also had numerous detractors, who pointed to the odd behavior of *ignis fatuus*, which seems to interact with or respond to the movements of the observer.

In recent years, British biologist Alan A. Mills attempted several experiments to replicate *ignis fatuus* in the laboratory. In one such study, Mills proposed that *ignis fatuus* may be cold flames; that is, luminescent arcs of light that appear when compounds are heated nearly to ignition point. They are bluish and without any discernible heat, suggestive of the 1971 incident in which a local woman claimed to put her hand through the blue light at Bachelors Grove. As of today, it is unclear whether such cold flames are found in nature. However, some substances that are known to produce them are, in fact, the product of organic decomposition, so there may be a possibility that decomposing matter on the grounds could be the source.

One of the most important contemporary researchers into *ignis fatuus* is Dr. Michael Persinger, whose Tectonic Strain Theory holds potentially massive import for the study of paranormal phenomena of every kind, from apparitional sightings to ghost lights to UFOs. Essentially, Persinger's theory suggests that the EM fields produced by strained bedrock—tectonic strain—can produce lights in the sky, ball lightning and "earth lights" or ghost lights and that these fields could also cause unstable conditions in the brain, leading to hallucinations that experiencers tend to interpret in terms of their cultural and learned knowledge and expectations. Persinger suggests, then, that some *ignis fatuus* may be geologic in origin, piezoelectrically created by these strains, which also heat up rock and vaporize the water they contain. Rock or soil containing something piezoelectric, like quartz, may also produce electricity, which could appear as something luminescent or interfere with the brain function of the witness, causing hallucinations. That is, experiencers could interpret both actual radiant effects and hallucinations as ghosts, religious apparitions or UFOs, depending on what they believe or expect.

For students of Bachelors Grove, Persinger's research is a lot to think about, especially by investigators who have wondered if something about the very land itself is the dynamo behind the myriad extraordinary phenomena of this site. The mysterious lights of Bachelors Grove, then, may be the most prolific of its phenomena because they may be the very foundation of them.

THE MADONNA OF BACHELORS GROVE

On August 10, 1991, Judy Huff-Felz was visiting Bachelors Grove Cemetery with the Ghost Research Society, one of the oldest local ghost-hunting groups in the nation. During that visit, she took one of the most controversial and infamous paranormal photos of all time, first published in the *Chicago Sun-Times* and the *National Examiner*: the incredible capture of the "Madonna of Bachelors Grove." The image of a "White Lady" or the "Woman on the Stone" has been circulated in all corners of the globe and regularly appears on lists of top paranormal photographs. It is a ritual for visitors to Bachelors Grove to reenact that renowned scene, having their photographs taken sitting on that stone.

Judy Huff-Felz first contacted me in the late 1990s to tell me about the day she took her famous photo, and I asked her to retell it here:

> *In the late '80s my sister and I convinced our mom to start a group which gave lessons on how to teach people how to find, enhance and safely use their abilities. After all of the sessions were over with each group my sister* [Mari Abba] *and I organized and ran an interactive ghost tour. This was for our mom's students to experiment and practice their abilities at several known haunted locations throughout Chicago and the suburbs.*
>
> *My sister and I met Dale Kaczmarek, founder of the Ghost Research Society. He invited us to his meetings and we then became members of his group. In 1991 GRS had planned an investigation for Bachelor's Grove*

Cemetery. The team members brought their equipment; my mom, sister and I were coming only with our gifts. Someone from the group suggested I bring some infrared film and take pictures of where I sensed activity.

The investigation was done where each member was given a clipboard, a pen and a map of the cemetery. Then everyone except for one person would wait outside of the fenced area. Then one person at a time would walk through Bachelors with our clipboard and whatever equipment they brought with them. As they walked around, they would note where and what they saw, heard and/or felt. Then they would use their equipment to see if they could detect something.

So as I walked through, I'd take pictures where I felt something. My camera was an Olympus automatic 35mm telephoto. As soon as you would take a picture, the camera would automatically wind the film to the next frame. The design of this camera made it impossible to double expose film. After developing my pictures, I found a woman or girl sitting on a broken piece of headstone. I did not see her with my naked eye the day of the investigation, although I believe I may have come across her on a few other occasions later.

The rest is history.

Without question, one of the most famous of paranormal manifestations at Bachelors Grove is that of this White Lady or Madonna of the Grove, a female figure in white, sometimes called "Mrs. Rogers" in local tellings of her story. The Madonna is described as a woman with dark hair, dressed in a long white dress or dressing gown. She has been reported walking through the cemetery, putting flowers on the graves, carrying a baby or "looking for her baby."

Origins of reports of this White Lady at Bachelors Grove have been largely unknown until now. After rigorous research, I can conclude that the earliest mention I have found that refers to a woman searching for a baby or holding a baby was on a 1977 radio show hosted by the late Chicago broadcaster Eddie Schwartz, during which a caller talked about capturing a photo of a "shrouded figure…carrying a baby." In the same segment, the caller refers to the image as "a nun…carrying a baby in white swaddling." The caller says she first thought she had captured a photo of "the Virgin Mary," as the figure was dressed "in a blue habitat [*sic*]…with white trim." I believe this testimony, broadcast to probably hundreds of thousands of listeners, is also the origin of references to a "Madonna" of Bachelors Grove.

Who is the Madonna of Bachelors Grove? There are many theories surrounding the identity of this mysterious woman in white.

In light of the many stories told about the old turnpike road and the days of joyriding and drinking parties, could she have been an ill-fated teenager who possibly drowned in the quarry pond or was killed in a car accident along the road? No news stories have surfaced regarding such an accident or death, but the possibility remains. Often, stories of "women in white" have begun after such "partying" accidents, as cautionary tales. But the truth of the matter here is up for debate.

A popular candidate for the Madonna of Bachelors Grove is Amelia Patrick, the first wife of Senator John Humphrey. Another sad infant death, the couple's child, little Libby May, was laid to rest with Amelia's family at Bachelors Grove, though Amelia was later interred elsewhere. Could Amelia be making nightly visits to the Grove in search of her separated child?

Two sisters-in-law emerge as candidates: Katherine Vogt Fulton and Luella Fulton Rogers. Katherine, who married Luella's brother Bert Fulton, was heartbroken by the loss of her child, little Marci May (formerly erroneously known as Marcia), who died in infancy. The young couple's baby was buried at the Fulton family lot in Bachelors Grove, under the famous Fulton stone, identified with the "Infant Daughter" marker. Local historians pass on the knowledge that, at the time of Marci May's death, the Fultons and the Vogts did not get along. Though the Vogt family owned space at Zion Lutheran Cemetery in Tinley Park, apparently the burial of a Fulton there was not an option, so John and Hulda offered burial at their family plot at Bachelors Grove. Years later, the child's parents were laid to rest in town, at Zion Lutheran Cemetery, with Katherine Vogt's kin. Could an otherworldly Katherine be searching for her baby, buried so far away and under such sad circumstances?

In folklore, a White Lady (also known as a *Mulher de Branco*) is a type of female ghost reportedly seen in rural areas and associated with some local legend of tragedy. Often, these women are supposed to have been killed in car accidents, such as Chicago's own "Resurrection Mary" or England's "Ghost of Blue Bell Hill." I strongly believe the best candidate for the Madonna to be Luella (or Lulu) Fulton Rogers, who was killed by a hit-and-run driver in 1937, reportedly the week after her sixtieth birthday, and who is buried at her family's lot at Bachelors Grove: the lot of John Jr. and Hulda Turney Fulton. Some believe that a resemblance seems to exist between Luella and the image in Judy Huff-Felz's famous photo. Moreover, Luella's baby sister, Emma, is also buried with her at the Fulton stone, but her marker was stolen long ago. When it was recovered, it was not returned to the Grove but, rather, placed into the care of the Tinley

Park Historical Society. Could Luella be upset that her sister's stone is missing? Is that what the spirit is looking for?

Old, local references refer to the Madonna as "Mrs. Rogers" and surely point to some connection to Luella. This would mean that it was contemporaries of Luella who started the story of the Woman in White at Bachelors Grove, making this the oldest ghost story at Bachelors Grove, originating in the 1930s. In light of all we now know, it seems likely that reported sightings of the ghost of Luella Fulton Rogers were what first drew young people to Bachelors Grove Cemetery to look for ghosts.

THE MAGIC HOUSE

Experiences of "vanishing houses"—usually believed to be evidence of time slips or "wrinkles in time"—have been told in many parts of the world and in many eras. Probably the most well known of these incidents became known as the Moberly-Jourdain incident, otherwise known as the Ghosts of *Petit Trianon*, which supposedly were experienced by Charlotte Anne Moberly and Eleanor Jourdain in Versailles, France, in the early twentieth century. During a visit to the *Petit Trianon*, a small house on the grounds of the Palace of Versailles, the two women claimed to have been transported to the site the way it looked in the eighteenth century and to have even seen buildings, a bridge and other structures that they could not have known about but that had been demolished years before. They also claimed to have seen the ghosts of Marie Antoinette and other prominent eighteenth-century characters. During the experience, the women said they felt an overpowering sense of oppression and a sinister feeling from the people and structures they encountered. They also described the scenery and its inhabitants as "flat and lifeless."

The pair became interested in the history of Versailles after their experience, and they soon returned to visit the Trianon gardens again, but they could not find the path they had walked. Nor could they locate the bridge they'd seen. Further, while the gardens had been nearly empty on their earlier visit, populated with just a few antiquely attired people, now they were filled with modern tourists. In 1911, the two women published their experiences in a book called *An Adventure*. Though the book was widely popular, the pair was roundly shamed by critics, including the illustrious Society for Psychical Research, which believed the two women had simply been mistaken about the preternatural aspect of what they had seen.

Rougham Green, in the English region of Suffolk, has for a century and a half hosted a phantom house. In 1860, a local farmer, Robert Palfrey, was baling hay on a summer evening when he felt a sudden chill on the warm night. He looked up to see a large, red brick house with lush gardens surrounding it, though no house existed in the area. Some years later, in 1912, Palfrey's grandson James Cobbold was driving a pony trap with the village butcher, George Waylett, when again the temperature plummeted and they heard a whooshing noise. The animal reared, throwing Waylett to the ground. There, in front of the men and the pony, had appeared a massive Georgian house, surrounded by beautiful blooming gardens, though a moment before there had been only a farm field and no structures of any kind. Seconds later, the house became enshrouded in mist—and then vanished again. The house would be seen again in 1926 when a young teacher and her pupil were walking through the area and came upon a huge house with a wall surrounding it and huge iron gates at the entrance. Returning home, the teacher—new to the area—inquired as to the residents of the grand home. She was informed that there was no such house in existence. Sure enough, when the pair returned to the site on another walk, they found the spot empty.

Even the Chicago area has vanishing houses outside of Bachelors Grove. In the northwest suburbs, Cuba Road is known as an extremely haunted tract that runs through old farms and country houses. A "vanishing house" that has been reported by travelers reportedly seems as real as can be but disappears in the rearview mirror or is gone upon a return visit.

Perhaps no vanishing house, however, is more well known in the annals of ghost lore than the "magic house" of Bachelors Grove.

Several years ago, Amelia Cotter, a dear friend of mine—also a longtime paranormal researcher and writer—had the experience of seeing the house, along with the group of ghost hunters accompanying her. To this day, the event keeps a dark hold on her, as she tells in this account:

> *In April 2009, I was at the cemetery after dark with a group of about eight people. After exploring quietly on our own, we were mysteriously drawn together near the entrance of the cemetery, where we made small talk until one of us noticed a round light glowing through the woods, in the direction of the path leading back to the road. We all observed this light, having not seen it earlier in the night. I stood wondering if the light was coming from a distant streetlight, a*

house on the other side of the woods, the moon or even an illuminated street sign. A few of us made similar remarks out loud as we then watched the light change shape.

It took on the form of a rectangular window with a cross-patterned wooden pane. Its glow was soft and evoked a sensation of reading by candlelight or low light. This cozy image was offset by a deep feeling of menace, the feeling of being violated and looked into by whatever it was that was creating this "window." The image developed further in my mind of a house around this window—an old-fashioned, classic-looking white house with a porch swing. Again, this normally benign image was extremely unsettling.

We decided to follow the light to see if we could find its origin. As if in a trance, we all got on the path and started walking away from the cemetery and toward the light. The light lost its window shape and became round again and seemed to move alongside us off in the distance. It danced up and down, getting higher and then lower and pulsating. It was thick enough for us to observe tree branches passing in front of it as it moved. For all our efforts to take photos, we could not capture it on film. None of us had video cameras and we just had regular digital cameras on us—the night was just meant to be an amateur outing for fun, and we weren't at all expecting something like this to happen!

Before we knew it, we were back out on the road. We filed quietly into our van and didn't speak of how strange it was that just moments earlier, we were totally fine exploring the cemetery, and now, all of a sudden, we had left. Like a deep-sea angler, this light had lured us out of the cemetery. It wasn't until I got home that I "snapped out of it." About two weeks later, we all got together again, and the others described a similar experience of realizing later what had truly happened but not giving it a second thought at the time.

I was deeply disturbed by this experience and the images of the window and house, and I had a hard time talking about them for a long time. Every time I would think about them, I would feel like whatever "it" was that caused this to occur was in my thoughts again and, as bizarre as it might sound, was pleased with this effect it had on me. As someone who has studied and experienced the supernatural for years, I could not place this phantom house experience into any neat and clean paranormal category. I do not feel that what happened to us was associated with the good people buried at the cemetery, but rather something darker, perhaps a combination of something already on the land and drawn to the cemetery and the years of desecration and rituals that have taken place there.

I feel more empowered to talk about it now that several years have passed. I've visited Bachelors Grove several times since this happened, and I know it's a very special place.

Amelia's account introduces many common motifs of the widely experienced house of Bachelors Grove, which has been seen by what can only be estimated to be hundreds of visitors, based on the nearly sixty eyewitness accounts I myself have gathered the past thirty years without really even soliciting them.

One is the style of the house. Every single account of the house describes it as a white farmhouse or farm-style house around one and a half stories tall—a simple frame house with a dormer or attic.

A second detail—that of the cross-paned window—is common to most every sighting. The window is the focal point, and many witnesses have seen only a window and no house or have photographed only a window and no house. Particular to the window is a light burning inside. Witnesses insist this light is "glowing" or "flickering." And some describe it as soft and golden and say that it is a natural firelight, not electric, although one woman who saw the house in the 1960s told Richard Crowe she'd thought it might have been light from a television set and remembered looking for cables that might have explained electricity in these isolated woods.

The porch swing mentioned by Amelia, too, is almost always mentioned in descriptions of the house, and some accounts even talk about it "swinging gently."

The feeling that the house is "leading" one somewhere, "attracting" one to it, is also almost universally prevalent in accounts. Walking toward it only to have it "shrink" or "get smaller and smaller" before disappearing is, similarly, overwhelmingly experienced.

Lastly, and most chillingly, the feeling of menace or malevolence from the house and the impression that some intelligence is taking pleasure in frightening or unnerving the witness are emotional effects shared by a majority of experiencers and are reminiscent of the experiences of the women at Versailles so many years ago.

It was commonly believed that no one had ever entered this magic house (or at least returned to tell about it). However, in 1997, soon after the publication of my first book, I gave a lecture at a library in the Bachelors Grove area and spoke to numerous patrons who had had experiences at the Grove earlier in their lives, including a man in his late seventies who had grown up exploring the woods surrounding Crestwood, his hometown. He told me that when he was a boy, he was playing in the woods near the cemetery with his friend sometime after 1940. This was a time by which the homes in the area had all been torn down. This particular afternoon, they had passed along the old turnpike and seen a house where a woman was waving to them from the porch. She was a grandmotherly woman, elderly but healthy looking, and she motioned for them to come closer. They walked up the front path, and when they got close enough to hear her, she said, "I just baked cookies. Come and have some!" Times being what they were, they went in and followed the woman through the modest farmhouse to the kitchen, where the smell of chocolate filled the cozy space. They sat with the woman and ate their fill of freshly baked cookies and drank coffee diluted with lots of milk and sugar. He did not recall what she talked about, if anything. When they finished, it was beginning to be sunset, so the boys said they had to go.

The next day, thinking of cookies, the boys headed back to the house, hoping for another invitation. But the house was gone.

Another story was told to me by a woman who had grown up in the area in the 1970s. She and two friends were walking down the old turnpike path near the creek one afternoon when they were startled to see a great gathering of people outside an old white farmhouse in a clearing in the woods. As she described it, there was a "long line of people, many of them dressed in long robe-like garments, standing quietly outside the door, as if queuing up for some event." They thought maybe it was some sort of independent church or "some kind of hippie thing," as it was the early '70s. Readers may note that this was around the same time that reports of ritual activity began to circulate regarding the cemetery and surrounding woods, and robed figures—both preternatural and flesh-and-blood—were being seen with increasing frequency. When the young woman returned with friends a few weeks later, the house they had seen was gone.

The late Richard T. Crowe, who grew up on the southwest side of Chicago, claimed to have collected dozens of drawings made by witnesses to the magic house, all showing a similar structure and style. A documentary he made featured interviews with two witnesses of the house who, as part of the program, showed similar drawings they had made of the house, allegedly with no previous knowledge of one another. Crowe also talked on the Eddie Schwartz radio show in 1976 about one witness who had seen the house and tried to get closer to it, knowing there was no house in the woods and realizing how unusual the situation was. He was running and had to push through some brambles and bushes, and he suddenly "found himself falling through the air. He had come upon the house, but it disappeared, and he ended up falling into the stone foundation of the house."

Some researchers have wondered if the house is the "ghost" of a home that once stood in the Grove—possibly even the phantom residue of one of the Schmidt family houses that stood off the turnpike road until the 1920s, when Margaretha Schmidt sold the property to the county. Certainly, the photographs of the Schmidt home or homes that have surfaced in recent years have fueled that theory, since witnesses have tended to describe a somewhat similar house. However, rarely is the magic house seen in this area. Most often, the house is seen either just past the cemetery and west of the old turnpike road or on the ravine of the creek by visitors walking between the cemetery and the creek near the quarry pond. As recently as 2015, the house was seen inside the cemetery itself by a driver passing over the quarry along 143rd Street, the new turnpike road. She was driving home from work just before sundown and, as she always did, glanced over to catch a look at the cemetery, which can be seen from the road, across the quarry. Though she had made this gesture probably hundreds of times, this time she saw a white frame house standing inside the cemetery. When she made a U-turn, however, to come back around and verify what she had seen, the house was gone.

In 2014, the house was actually photographed standing just past the tree line outside the cemetery gates, just south of "the Path." Appearing to be a white frame house built on posts, the photograph—taken by Karl K—also captured the image of what appears to be a male figure walking across the path.

In the 1960s, several witnesses saw the house in this same area. One such witness said she and her date were driving down the path toward the cemetery one stormy night and saw the house to the south of the path and a man with a lantern talking to the people in the car ahead of them, motioning for them to turn back and leave the area. When they returned some weeks later, the house was gone.

Intriguingly, cooking smells have also been reported in these same areas, especially along the creek, where local residents Bill and Cheri Swinford smelled chocolate cookies or brownies baking one afternoon. On another occasion, a group of ghost hunters was at the "Keebler Tree" or "Holy Tree" using a spirit box (used to attempt electronic communication with entities) when they all began to smell Italian food cooking, including a strong odor of garlic. On yet another occasion, a visitor smelled barbecue cooking. Unlike normal cooking or baking smells, these smells are there one moment and gone the next.

There were other houses here in the area, as we shall see, including two others whose inhabitants are now known, and both had strong ties to the cemetery. Of this, more later.

Astonishingly, the Swiss psychiatrist Carl Jung had his own "vanishing" incident during the 1930s, when he traveled to the town of Ravenna, the former capital of the Western Roman Empire. Jung was quite taken with the history of a certain Roman princess and was very excited about visiting her tomb in town. After the visit, he and his travel companion went on to the Neonian Baptistery, an open building illuminated by four large clear paned windows. Finishing their visit, the pair returned to Switzerland.

Twenty years later, Jung returned to Ravenna and experienced what he would describe as "among the most curious events of my life." His impressions of the visit were described in Aniela Jaffe's *Memories, Dreams, and Reflections*. Jung remembered the "strange mood" he fell under during his second visit to the tomb and, amazingly, recounted a "mild blue light" that filled the room of the baptistery when he again entered. He later reflected that, for some reason, he was not troubled by the fact of this light, though it had no apparent source. What *was* startling, however, was the fact that—where the four great windows had been—there were now four enormous mosaics depicting aquatic events in the life of the Church, including the parting of the Red Sea, the baptism of Jesus on the Jordan and others. Jung and his companion viewed these wondrous mosaics for some time before departing.

During his time in Ravenna and later, Jung attempted to purchase photographs of the mosaics from firms that specialized in architectural photographs of prominent buildings but discovered, to his shock, that the mosaics did not exist and never had.

Jung's travel companion was equally astounded to discover that what they had both seen was not really *real* and for years insisted that there must be some mistake, but there was not. There were, in fact, four clear windows in the baptistery and no mosaics of any kind. Nor had there ever been.

Incredibly, Jung *did* discover that his revered princess, during a treacherous ocean crossing, had made a vow that if she survived she would build a church at Ravenna in thanksgiving and decorate it with artwork showing God's power over the sea. Safely home, she kept her vow and built the Basilica of San Giovanni, adorned in mosaics, which was eventually obliterated by fire.

Deeply puzzled and fascinated by his experience, Jung attempted to understand what had happened. After many considerations, he could only conclude that his unconscious mind may have created a vision, based on his "very strong kinship, culturally and spiritually, with the princess" and his "immersion in the total identification with the princess."

Could this be what happens at Bachelors Grove? Certainly, many visitors feel a "very strong kinship, culturally and spiritually," with the history and people of the Grove. Are these appearances merely creative expressions of the viewer, powered by this strong kinship? Or are visitors tapping the psyches and realities of those long gone and actually seeing the world through their eyes?

And what about the blue light that accompanied Jung's vision? Considering the famed blue lights that often preface apparitions of Bachelors Grove's magic house, there may be much here to consider.

THE CARETAKER OR LANTERN MAN

In the 1960s, a local couple was driving toward Bachelors Grove Cemetery on the path and saw a man with a lantern at the cemetery entrance motioning for them to turn back and leave the area. Just south of the path, right near the cemetery gate, was a frame house at the edge of the woods.

A similar man was seen by three young women visiting the cemetery one afternoon many years later, in the first decade of the 2000s. They had traveled the old turnpike road on foot back to the cemetery one afternoon, and as they passed the bend in the road, they saw ahead of them, at the cemetery gate, an elderly man holding an oil lantern and motioning for them to come more quickly, as if they should hurry. The women thought there was a tour starting and quickened their pace as the man went ahead into the gate and passed from their sight. When they reached the cemetery, however, the man had vanished. No one at all was in the burying ground or anywhere nearby.

Others tell of experiences in the 1970s during which they encountered a man with a lantern and sometimes a gun on the ravine or at the cemetery gate, who told them in no uncertain terms to get out. However, when reassured that they meant no harm, that they were only there in search of the "disappearing house," the man told them that it was very real and that he would show it to them. Walking behind them and pointing the way, he would vanish en route. One witness claims to have seen this "lantern man" walk right through a tree as he approached him through the woods near the path.

Gloria Maranda saw a man with a lantern on several occasions in the mid-1960s, including one occasion when she and her companions had a confrontation with him:

> *I grew up on the southwest side of Chicago, on 69th and Hamlin. We used to go to different haunted spots just for a thrill or scare. Although I've heard Bachelors Grove was a makeout spot for some, we never went for that. We usually went in a group—sometimes couples or not—and we would usually stop at Dog 'n' Suds or A&W on the way, since you had to go when it was dark for the fog to set in. It was always foggy there at about nine or so when we got there. We usually went in summer and on a Saturday night. Friday night was reserved for the teen dances at all the local parishes. I was about sixteen or seventeen. So that would have been '66 or '67. The first time I saw the caretaker was when I was sixteen. We would go there and just look at the cemetery hoping to see orbs or ghosts. We sometimes could hear noises like rustling of leaves or someone walking, but no one was there.*
>
> *Well this one night was really warm and humid; all the car windows were open. As we watched the cemetery, we could see the figure of a man who looked like he was glowing in the dark. He had a lantern-type light in his hand, and he was in the distance next to a shack of some kind. The guys we were with got really brave and wanted to go see who he was, so they got out of the car and approached the fence. The gate was broken, and it was no problem for them to get through. We girls stayed in the car with two other guys. The girls were scared, but it was too hot to roll up the windows. The caretaker figure moved toward us as the boys were at the gate. He then raised his lantern and walked closer. We could hear chains dragging and rattling as he walked. I can remember this because all of us said it reminded them of Scrooge's partner's ghost in the movie* Christmas Carol, *the way they clanked. He walked toward the boys and held out the lantern and said, "Get out of here if you know what's good for you and don't come back!"*
>
> *The boys ran back to the car, and they were about fifty feet from him at that time and the car was about another few feet from the fence. The caretaker sounded like an old mean man, but we still couldn't see his face. He just glowed in the light, but he had a yellow rain slicker and hat on, which was odd, because it hadn't been raining. When the boys got back in*

the car, we took off like a bat out of hell and didn't go back for over a year! I do remember he had a limp and sort of dragged one leg, but the noise from the chains definitely happened when he moved.

That was the only time we actually had an interaction with him; after that we might see him in the far distance, always with his light and always with the yellow rain slicker. He would go into the shack sometimes and other times just walk around.

The shack was small, the size of a backyard shed. Sometimes you could see a light in the small window, but it was farther into the cemetery, maybe even in the forest preserves. But many people I have talked to said the shack never existed. I only know I saw it every time we went. And I really thought at the time we saw the caretaker that lived there.

This intriguing account introduces elements from another phenomenon at Bachelors Grove: the so-called Yellow Man, who is described as wearing a yellow or golden suit and hat and as "glowing" or "translucent," of which more later. Were Maranda's encounters those of a real caretaker or of something paranormal? What was the "shack" she and her companions saw, so many years after the removal of all the area structures? And what was the source of the clanking and dragging of chains they heard?

Sometimes this Caretaker of Bachelors Grove is described as a "one-armed sniper" or a "one-armed man." This is interesting, since the legend of the "Hooked Maniac" is one that has been told about this spot for years.

Cemetery trustee Clarence Fulton insisted there never was a "caretaker" of the cemetery in the traditional sense. He claimed that the cemetery, as a local settlers' burying ground, was cared for by landowners in the area during the time of farming and by trustees of the cemetery throughout the larger part of the twentieth century, until the cemetery's condemnation in 1976. In fact, however, there were several "caretakers" of the cemetery, as unofficial as they might have been.

Certainly, Fulton himself could be described as nothing but a caretaker. He was a member of the private board of trustees of the cemetery, the go-to person for reporters and others when the cemetery was in the news, and he also was the one to suggest the creation of a Bachelors Grove "shrine." If Fulton didn't think of himself as the caretaker of the cemetery, he was likely alone in that thought. Don't forget, too, that Fulton was known for hiding in the cemetery to scare away would-be vandals and that he plainly told reporters that his companion in these night watches carried a gun. Surely, numerous 1960s-era reports were real encounters with Fulton. Did he perhaps wear a slicker and hat colored with luminous paint to try to "scare" kids away? Did he rig up some chains to add to the "spooky" effect?

It also seems fair to argue that the mysterious Huburt Geist was a self-appointed caretaker of the cemetery, taking it upon himself to chase away young ne'er-do-wells and their shenanigans by any means necessary. Of course, he himself said he would carry a lantern on his nighttime escapades through Bachelors Grove. At least some of the sightings in the 1930s and '40s were surely of this very real person.

But what of the more recent sightings of a caretaker or "lantern man" at Bachelors Grove? Could one of these old night watchmen have remained here after death to watch over the cemetery? Could it be Fulton or Geist? Or even someone else?

In recent years, another possibility for a caretaker's identity has come to light. In 1996, Brad Bettenhausen of the Tinley Park Historical Society published a letter he had received from Jan Doan of Claremont, Illinois, about her family, the Hardys, a prominent Bachelors Grove name.

Doan's father had lived at the corner of 147th Street and Ridgeland as a child. Her grandfather was Fred Hardy, who emigrated from Lincolnshire, England, in 1886 with his brother Albert. Two of their sisters also migrated to the area later. Edna Wright Hardy was Fred and Albert's mother. She lived in Lincolnshire her whole life and had seventeen children with her husband, Henry Hardy. After his death, Edna visited her children in America in 1893 to attend the World's Fair in Chicago. Upon her return to England, she married William Sanderson. After his death, she again visited with her children in America, in the fall of 1906, but became too ill to return to England. She died in Bremen Township and was buried at Bachelors Grove. Edna's mother was originally interred there as well but was reinterred in town, at Zion Lutheran, where the rest of the family reposes. Edna remains at Bachelors Grove alone, in a grave originally owned by her son Albert.

A map showing the homesteaders of 1900 held by the Tinley Park Historical Society shows that the southwest end of the cemetery marked the edge of the Schmidt land and the beginning of the land occupied (but not necessarily owned) by Albert Hardy. In Doan's letter, she speaks fondly of the Hardy house "across the crick" where her uncle Albert lived. She says that she visited Bachelors Grove Cemetery "at least twice a month from spring to fall for many years. My dad and grandpa would cut the grass around the graves, trim the hedge, plant and water flowers and, in general, take care of the area." Though it actually stood across the creek, could Albert's house somehow be the magic house seen by numerous witnesses along the old road?

Yet another interesting caretaker candidate dwells on the ravine, where many visitors have encountered the phantom house and caretaker. This, we have seen, is where Christ Boehm lived and operated his quarry. From the court transcripts over the Boehm property, it seems hardly likely that Boehm had any passionate attachment to this land. The quarry seems to have been a catch-as-catch-can operation, with witnesses saying it was often closed. Boehm had no wife or children and seems to have been something of a drifter, ending up in Knox, Indiana, during the time of the forest preserve upheaval. None of his family lived at the Grove, living and working in Worth and Chicago. Though he fought the sale of the land in court—extensively and at great expense to the county—his interest was in getting more money, not in any apparent love for the land. Interestingly, however, at the court hearing regarding his land, Boehm's house was described as being "built on posts," much like the house in Karl K's photo. And many visitors have seen the house in the area of the quarry, both on the ravine and in the cemetery itself.

It seems possible that the Boehm house was formerly a home built by the Everdens when they arrived in the area in the 1830s. Very old plat maps of the area show a structure in this location when they owned the land, and in the court transcript of 1927, Boehm said that his house had been rebuilt from a much older house, probably built by the Everdens. It would certainly be easy to believe in a supernatural bond between the very first owners of this land and the sightings today.

An intriguing aspect of the Caretaker sightings is that there have been numerous occasions when the Caretaker beckoned to visitors or invited them to come into the woods or the cemetery, rather than shooing them away. Once again, the apparition "lures" the visitor in, just as the magic house and the lights reportedly do. Like the house, some wonder if these Caretaker apparitions are malevolent entities in disguise, tricking visitors to come inside, and more deeply under their spell, by appearing as what visitors want to see.

THE YELLOW MAN, THE SUIT MAN, THE HAT MAN AND THE TALL MAN

In the mid-1980s, local paranormal researcher Norman Basile was visiting Bachelors Grove Cemetery overnight with a colleague when he saw, standing near a tree, a man in a suit and hat, with a yellowish cast to his figure.

As Basile attempted to take a photograph, the man vanished. Earlier the same year, Basile had been investigating with a fellow researcher when his colleague claimed to have seen a figure lit up by a yellow glow, wearing a suit and hat. As they both stared at the site, a nearby tree began to shake frantically, and streaking red lights shot through the air. The two hightailed it out, both deeply shaken.

Years later, in the early 2000s, Nina Jankowski was investigating near the Shields lot in the northeast quadrant of the cemetery when she felt faint. In her peripheral vision she saw a shadowy figure run past her. Nina quickly snapped a photograph. It was then that Nina noticed that the camera had turned itself on and set itself to a different setting than the one she'd been using.

During one of my first years investigating the Grove, I encountered a woman who had visited the cemetery in 1982 at night and glimpsed a man in a "golden suit" standing near this same stone, who disappeared "in a shower of sparkly red lights" a moment later. She recalled that, just before the incident, she had felt a "prickly wave" over her skin and that the hair on her arms stood on end for about a minute after the incident.

Joining this rather ethereal "yellow man" or "yellow suit man" is a very real-looking man in a vintage-style suit who has been seen by and even interacted with visitors. In the very early spring of 2015, the great Chicago crime historian Richard Lindberg invited me to assist as a cohost on a bus tour sponsored by the Chicago History Museum. After a wonderful afternoon, we said our goodbyes and headed to the parking lot. I was stopped by one of the tour guests, who asked if I was, in fact, the lady who specialized in Bachelors Grove. I said that, yes, it is a special interest of mine, and he began his story. I assumed this would be the usual: "My friends and I were out there one night, drinking, in the '60s or '70s..." But this was a very different story.

The gentleman told me that he had served in the Gulf War in the 1990s and had come home very distraught and depressed. PTSD set in, and he felt no way out of the prison of his thoughts. He had gone into Bachelors Grove one afternoon with a length of rope to hang himself, reasoning in his despair that a cemetery would be a good place for this act. He rigged up a noose in one of the older oak trees near the old turnpike path and climbed up, slipping off the bough to finish the deed. The next thing he knew, he was quite awake, lying on the ground beneath the tree. The rope he'd used had been cut by a knife, and standing over him was a man wearing a brown suit and fedora, "like from another time," asking, "Are you okay?" The man on the ground was stunned, but he nodded, after which the stranger pointed toward the path and said, "They're looking for you!"

The man got up and stumbled toward the path, where he found police officers who had been dispatched after receiving a mysterious phone call about trouble near the cemetery. When he turned to thank the man, he found that he had disappeared without a trace, without a sound and with no possible way of leaving unseen. Reflecting on this later, he realized that there was no way the man who found him could have cut him down, left the cemetery, found a house, called 911 and returned to the cemetery in the short time he would have been unconscious. Further, no one in the area had allowed anyone to use their phone to make a call. The incident was half-jokingly written off as a product of "a guardian angel," but the man to this day wonders if it was just that.

Wendy Moxley Roe was there on a muddy day in April when she and Bill Swinford watched a well-dressed man, carrying a briefcase and a cell phone, walk toward the creek and never come back. And in late fall 2015, a group of bird watchers was taking photographs of migrating birds near the pond on a brisk afternoon when they saw a man dressed in a tropic weight suit, straw hat and white patent shoes come ambling along the pond bank, cross the cemetery and turn down the path toward the creek, never to return.

About 8:00 a.m. on a blustery, Saturday March morning in the early 1990s, a local man named Michael Malley was walking through the creek bed with a metal detector when he saw a young woman walk across the stony bed and into the woods about fifty feet ahead, dressed in a knee-length dark business suit and stepping carefully, wearing high-heeled shoes, with no coat or jacket except the suitcoat, no purse or bag and no one accompanying her. She did not acknowledge him, and though he spent about another hour and a half in the area, he never saw her again.

Strangest of all, in the early 2000s, a young local woman named Maggie Swinford was hiking along a trail near the path when she saw a pair of men's black shoes (only shoes) walk across the path ahead of her, disappearing into the woods beyond.

This experience of seeing well-dressed men—and sometimes women, and sometimes only shoes—walk into the woods at Bachelors Grove with its overgrown trails covered in brambles and thorns, often impassably muddy or even covered in snow, never to return, is a common and baffling one. A demonologist once told me that a common practice of demons in North America is to take the form of "corporate" apparitions: men or women in well-cut business attire, pristinely groomed. Whenever I hear a story about a well-dressed person at the Grove who vanishes, I think about this and about the many researchers who believe that evil spirits were conjured at the Grove during ritual activity dating to the 1960s, '70s and '80s.

Modern paranormal investigators have isolated a type of entity or energy called "The Hat Man," who is believed to be one specific type of Shadow Person. Often these apparitions are described as dark humanoids who appear to be wearing a fedora or top hap and usually a suit or trench coat. The Hat Man is generally thought to be associated with evil or negative events or energies.

Heidi Hollis, a researcher who coined the terms "Shadow People" and "Hat Man," reports that this dark entity tends to follow bloodlines through generations and to love places full of tragedy and, especially, ritual activity:

> *The Hat Man can follow bloodlines or anyone at all....He's known to romp in certain areas and known among native people to harass for generations, around the globe. But he is as pure evil as they come, so just when you think he follows rules, he doesn't. In areas where lots of bloodshed has happened, he can be more likely to appear...tragedy, pain, depression, dark magic...he loves it. Speak of him too much and he will be near, too. He's quite dangerous and always listening.*

Hollis has also documented many instances of Hat Man sightings in which witnesses describe the man as having glowing eyes. In an investigation of Bachelors Grove in the mid- 2000s by author Scott Markus and his team, the group was intrigued to find pairs of glowing lights that showed up on their infrared cameras but not to the naked eye or regular cameras. Upon further research, I found that numerous visitors have encountered what appeared to be "glowing eyes"—at the level of human eyes—in the darkness, often surrounded by dark forms or humanoid figures, usually in the woods or on the banks of the quarry pond.

The modern-day "meme" of Slender Man is one that has had a massive impact on storytelling and folk belief in our Internet age. The chilling tale of a tall, slender humanoid who stalks children has even driven several people to violence and murder, such as in the 2014 case of two Wisconsin girls, Anissa Weier and Morgan Geyser, who planned to kill a classmate and then walk to the Nicolet National Forest, where they believed Slender Man lived, to let him know of their act. But while Slender Man himself is a modern creation, the character does have some origins in numerous actual folk traditions.

In ancient folklore, some fairies were portrayed as gangly, well-dressed giants who would lead travelers off their paths to their doom. Often, they were known to be able to hypnotize people for this purpose. These creatures were known to punish humans who got too close to their business or spent too much time in their lairs. In Germany, the legend of the Erlking told of a tall man living in the forest whose aim was to lure children away from their parents. In Scotland, Fear Dubh ("The Black Man") was known to haunt forest paths at night, preying on children who wandered off alone. Northern Englanders lived in fear of the Clutchbone: a seven-foot monster who would dismember and burn victims he found alone in the woods. Like many of these phenomena, the Clutchbone was said to appear during electrical storms and to be accompanied by ball lightning or ghost lights.

Around the same time the Slender Man meme became popular, reports of a "Tall Man" returned to Bachelors Grove. Recall that in the 1970s, visitors to the Grove were coming out of the woods with the first reports of a "seven-foot giant" and that there was, in fact, a seven-foot-tall *living* man who would frequent the Grove, dressed in ceremonial robes, which either spawned or supported the ghost story. In recent years, however, actual photographs of what appears to be a very tall (eight- or nine-foot) man in a suit and sometimes a hat have been captured, usually in the northeast quadrant of the cemetery, near The Pines. Karl K, an avid researcher of the Grove, has taken several photos of this figure, in which the figure towers over the fence, which is at least seven feet high.

Once again, is something at Bachelors Grove taking the form of a popular figure in modern ghost stories to lure people to the area? If so, for what reason?

THE DOGS

Phantom dogs are found throughout the folklore of both the British Isles and Germany, so it is not surprising that they have found their way into the reports of Bachelors Grove, settled first by English migrants from New England and then by German immigrants. Throughout international lore, these dogs are almost always associated with death and, usually, evil. Often, sightings occur in tandem with electrical storms, and they are said to be seen most often at crossroads or along ancient spiritual roads. That the black dogs of Bachelors Grove are usually seen at the cemetery entrance is interesting, given the local folklore that says a portal opening exists there, or at the roped-off entrance to the path, since the old turnpike road was a Native American trail. Often Native Americans would lay down trails over lines in the landscape they believed to be of spiritual significance. Also interesting is the fact that the nearby cell towers—and possibly high EM fields—on the new turnpike are often pointed to as a possible source of the manifestations at the Grove. Could electricity really have something to do with these manifestations? Also important for Grove lore is the fact that phantom dogs have often been tied in folklore to instances in which humans sold their souls to the Devil. That the phantom dog tales began during the height of reports of ritual activity at the Grove is worth pointing out.

The earliest reports of phantom dogs at Bachelors Grove date from the 1980s, when the first published accounts appeared in books of American ghost lore. According to an early account, two men visiting the cemetery first saw strange lights in the bushes of the cemetery grounds and then what appeared to be the backside of a dog, which then faded away. Other similar sightings have been reported to me that occurred in the late 1990s and early 2000s. One young woman was visiting Bachelors Grove for the first time with two companions on a spring afternoon in 2002. As they walked south on the path and neared the cemetery, they saw a black Doberman standing near the gate, facing them. All three women saw the dog clearly at first, but as they got closer, the dog began to become blurry and transparent, until they could actually see the road on the other side of the animal. No one spoke until the dog had vanished entirely, and afterward all three said they had felt a strange calm or malaise come over them, as if they were temporarily drugged or hypnotized. Interestingly, they also reported that the hair on their arms stood on end for several minutes after the incident.

Most sightings seem to center on this cemetery entrance or on the roped-off entrance to the old turnpike road—the path—at 143rd Street. Visitors will sometimes see the dog standing at the roped entry as they cross the street toward it. Others have claimed that a dog blocked their way or followed them out as they walked up the path toward 143rd Street. Longtime paranormal researcher Jim Gracyzk is one witness who experienced a phantom dog in this way:

> *It was late, just a little past midnight on a warm summer night back in the late '80s. I was with one of my old school buddies and two of his co-workers who had just got off work. We were out driving around and looking*

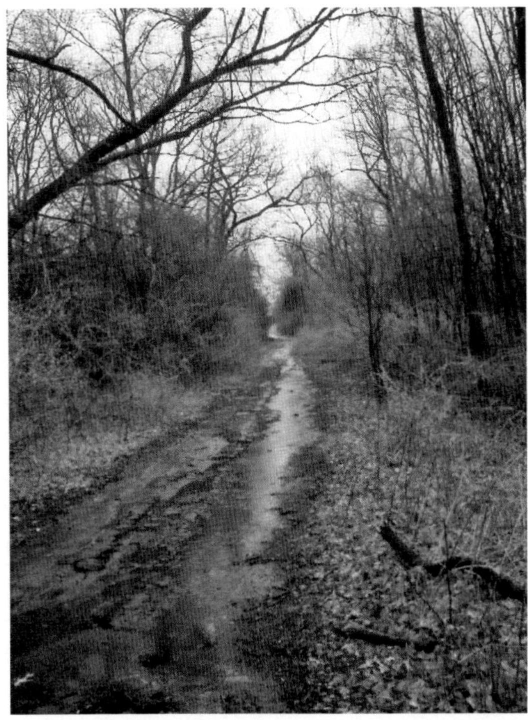

The old turnpike path hosts many strange phenomena, including the sighting of mysterious dogs, phantom cars and houses, voices, footsteps and lights. *Karl K.*

for something to do. None of us had even been to Bachelors Grove at night, so I drove on out there.

We parked the car a block or so down the turnpike by the houses on the side street. The streets were quiet, but we knew we had to keep a watchful eye out for the local police making their rounds. As we parked the car, we all agreed we go in together, we come out together—no matter what. This was a small verbal pact among four teenage guys. As the four of us kept a watchful eye out for cars, we ran and made it to the path down to Bachelors Grove.

Now this being the first time at night to Bachelors Grove, the other three guys relied on me to lead and get them back to the cemetery. As we walked through the woods down the trail, it seemed like the trail kept getting longer and longer. After a few minutes, we could see off on the right the outline of the fence to the cemetery.

Once we walked into the cemetery, it seemed peaceful and pretty quiet. We walked together within eyesight of one another and kept our voices down as we prowled around the cemetery. Everyone was amazed that we made it there, and the moonlight lit the cemetery rather well. After a few minutes of wandering around and nothing happening, we decided we better get back to the car before the cops showed up.

As I was leading everyone out of the cemetery, we were sort of bunched up and then started to stagger down the road, as each kept an eye out for anyone and, of course, the police. While I was leading, I saw up in front of me in the distance some kind of shape pacing back and forth on the trail and back into the woods. I asked, "Did anyone else see that?" and of course everyone else was trying to figure it out. We stopped and came up with a plan: to grab something like a good-size stick or a rock to protect oneself in case needed. We had all kept an eye out for people and cars, and now we have something in front of us. Slowly, we proceeded forward toward the cabled-off entrance. As we got closer, we could see it was a dog. Now our minds started to race: was this a wild dog or something?

Each step closer to the entrance we could see this dog more clearly. It was rather fat, like an adult-size black and brown looking Rottweiler. The dog was pacing back and forth, from about the middle of the trail to the side into the woods. The dog would walk out, sniff and turn back and go back into the woods. Ok, I thought, if we stick to the left side of the trail, keep an eye out, maybe the dog will just let us out. As we got close to the cable entrance, the dog was standing off into the woods as if letting us proceed. We bunched up and slowly walked past the dog. I remember, I glanced at the dog to see where it was, and I clearly could see it was black and tan, almost like a junkyard guard dog. The dog's eyes were dark, and amazingly, it just kept watching us walk by. All four of us kept watching back, checking to see where this dog was, still in the woods off the trail. We made it to the street on the pavement and then saw the dog step out of the woods and walk behind us to the edge of the trail to the pavement. We were already walking super-fast, almost running, not to draw the dog to chase us. Someone said, "The dog is still by the trail near the pavement" and said, "Run to the car." All of us dropped our sticks and rocks and ran to the car. Once we got to the car and were safe inside, everyone started talking.

We started the car up and of course had to go back down the turnpike to see where this dog was at now. Amazingly, we couldn't find the dog. The dog was nowhere to be seen by the road or entrance to the trail. We all laughed and were talking about how it was a close call on the way out. We couldn't figure out why we weren't chased by the dog and why it let us out of the trail.

Nobody brought up that night ever again, and I haven't seen any of those guys in years. None of them know I am into the paranormal, and if I ever cross paths with them, I would ask them about Bachelors Grove at night

> *and that dog by the trail. I am sure each one would tell you the story on how we got let out and just watched by a dog.*
>
> *Over the years, as I got into the paranormal in the late '90s and started doing research, I learned about a phantom dog. These phantom dogs are known to guard sacred places and keep an eye on things. I know what I saw that night, and it seemed real to all of us, but was it one of these dogs? None of us disrespected Bachelors Grove Cemetery that night, and we just went there out of curiosity. Was it* [because of] *the respect we paid to the departed ones and sacred site that we also were granted respect and able to leave in one piece out of the area?*

Local resident Bill Swinford was walking on the path toward the cemetery in April 2013 when he saw a black dog walking ahead and turning into the cemetery. He pulled back, keeping his own dog on a short leash (though his animal did not seem to react to the stranger), but when he reached the cemetery gates, the dog was gone. There was a mother in the cemetery with her children, and when he asked the woman where the dog went, she and the children assured him that they had seen no dog.

On another occasion, Swinford came out of the cemetery with his dog, Bailey, one winter afternoon and crossed into the Rubio Woods area across the new turnpike. They saw a stranger sitting on a log, accompanied by a black dog. Bailey did not react in any way to the stranger's dog, and when Swinford returned down the path a few minutes later, he found that the stranger's dog had left no prints in the snow.

Curiously, the sighting of one or another phantom dog is one of the rare phenomena at the Grove that tends to not be witnessed by everyone present. Typically, only one person or a fraction of those present see the dog, while their companions do not. Also, in about half of the experiences, the dog vanishes or becomes fainter before vanishing. In the other incidents, the dog disappears while witnesses are not looking in its direction or walks into the cemetery and vanishes while out of eyesight. These details seem evocative of the magic house experiences, in which witnesses have either seen the house "fade away" or find that the house has disappeared since they earlier passed the site of it.

Also common to numerous experiences are the appearance of small "dancing" lights at the time of the dog's appearance. Numerous phenomena at the Grove seem to occur in the presence of such lights, and it makes me wonder if, indeed, there is a portal or dimensional doorway here—whether there is some sort of static charge being emitted at the moment of transference between worlds.

THE CARS

Robert Patterson is a lifelong resident of Chicago's southwest side and has been visiting Bachelors Grove since his youth. He's a great documentarian of the Grove and took some of the oldest known photographs of the site. Though he says he has been here innumerable times, he has not had many paranormal experiences in the cemetery, but the road outside it is a different story:

> *Really, I've been at B.G. hundreds of times since 1976...never seen or heard anything. But I have witnessed things outside of the cemetery just driving by. On one occasion my brother Mike and I were driving on 143rd Street from Ridgeland Avenue. It was on Friday just after Thanksgiving around ten years ago. It was dusk, still light out, cloudy. We observed a dark minivan parked at the entrance* [to the old turnpike road]. *I was on the passenger side looking at the minivan, and there was no one inside. I said, "Boy, they're going to get a ticket!" After we passed, a few seconds later I looked in the passenger-side rear mirror and the minivan was gone, and there were no cars on the road at all.*

Possibly the most prolific of all Bachelors Grove phenomena is that of these phantom cars or ghost cars, which have been seen near the cemetery since at least the 1970s.

The late Chicago ghost hunter Richard Crowe himself saw one of the cars on two separate occasions, as he shared with listeners on the *Eddie Schwartz Show* in the 1970s.

Veteran broadcaster Ronald Smith recalls an incident that occurred in the early 1970s concerning the cars, which featured numerous vehicles at once:

> *In the fall of 1972, I was a student at North Central College in Naperville. As program director of the campus radio station, WONC-FM, I thought it would be a good idea to create a short radio program concerning local legends to air on Halloween evening. The show ended up being called "Journey to the Macabre," which was admittedly rather sensationalistic. As part of the program, a group of three of us from the station traveled to some of the sites, including Resurrection Cemetery, St. Rita Church and Bachelors Grove. Though we brought audio equipment, the tape consisted of us describing the sites and our "feelings." Since electronic voice phenomena was virtually unheard of, most of the audio went unused and even unexamined, replaced*

by a later phone conversation with Chicago ghost hunter Richard Crowe. I do remember Richard asking if we had seen the cabin in the woods—a relatively new phenomenon. We had not. But talk of it was the highlight of the show.

Having never been to the cemetery before, we approached from the east on Midlothian Turnpike. In those days, the road to the cemetery was open to cars (even at night) and ended in a large turnaround at its entrance. I remember the spooky sensation the overhanging trees gave to the short drive but mostly was concerned with the idea that the path was too narrow for two cars to safely pass. When we arrived at the turnaround, we were not even sure we were in the right place—the small cemetery was so decrepit and overgrown. A decision was made to exit and travel farther down the road in case we had made a wrong turn. When we got back to Midlothian Turnpike and continued heading west, I glanced out the back window (I was alone in the back seat) and saw around six cars turning down the path we had just left. I wish I could say there was something memorable about the cars, but it was dark and I certainly had no need to remember what they looked like—so I thought. Announcing to my friends that we must have been in the right place, we continued on to Ridgeland Avenue and headed back.

Turning back down the path toward the cemetery, I was now even more concerned about its narrowness. What if the cars that had preceded us decided to turn around and come back out? There would be no way to get around them. I wasn't sure there would even be enough room for all the cars to park in the turnaround. My fears were allayed, however, when we got to the entrance. We were alone.

Of course I wondered where the line of cars had gone. There shouldn't have been enough time for them to travel to the cemetery and leave again. But logic dictated that must have been the case, and I put it out of my mind. We did the investigation, created the program and life moved on.

However, in the mid-'90s, I had an opportunity to speak again with Richard Crowe, who mentioned the existence of ghost cars on Midlothian Turnpike. Almost offhandedly, he also spoke of ghost cars and even a ghostly funeral procession seen on the old road that once ran past the cemetery, which rang a bell with me. I'm not saying what I saw that night in 1972 was a funeral cortege, but it might have been an explanation to the mystery that I remembered still twenty-plus years later.

Phantom cars are not exclusive to Bachelors Grove. In Lanikai, Hawaii, motorists have reported seeing a mysterious black car that disappears and reappears again seconds later. In the early 1980s, a British driver literally crashed his car on the side of the road to avoid making contact with a truck barreling toward him, which suddenly vanished. Also in Britain, at St. Marks Road and Cambridge Garden in Ladborke Grove, locals have long told of a ghost bus that caused numerous accidents over many years, including one that proved fatal. Even in the Chicago area, there are other reports of phantom cars, including on notorious Bloods Point Road, Cherry Valley Road and Cuba Road in the Northwest suburbs and even at Rosehill Cemetery, where a phantom SUV has been seen by numerous visitors in recent years.

Some researchers have claimed that these phantom cars at Bachelors Grove may be tied to the alleged dumping of bodies by gangland criminals in the 1920s and '30s, but I have never found an incident in which the automobiles seen were of that vintage. The vehicles have ranged from 1960s and '70s vans to '70s sedans to a 1980s "low rider" outfitted with detailing and fancy rims. One woman reported seeing a horse and buggy turn into the road ahead of her on 143rd Street.

The Farmer

One of the most well-known ghost stories of Bachelors Grove is also one with few documented witnesses. Since the late 1970s or early 1980s, the story has circulated of a phantom farmer and plow horse seen on or near the new Midlothian Turnpike (143rd Street). According to the story, this is the apparition of a local farmer who was plowing his land near the quarry in the 1870s when the horse either became frightened and bolted or simply got too close to the quarry edge, pulling in both farmer and plow and drowning them. According to local legend, because of the depth of the quarry, the bodies and plow were never recovered.

Two incidents have been publicly shared by witnesses to this apparition, including one dating to the 1970s in which two local law-enforcement officers saw a farmer driving his plow and horse up out of the quarry pond and across 143rd Street, disappearing into Rubio Woods across the road.

Local researchers claimed to have found newspaper accounts of the rumored accident, but none ever became public. I myself combed every newspaper archive and search engine for years to try to track down the story, but with no success whatsoever. Even the origins of the quarry and all trace of it in the public record remained a mystery. Not even the local historical societies knew anything about it.

Then, in the winter of early 2016, I came upon an extraordinary document in the archives of the Forest Preserve District of Cook County: a 115-page court hearing transcript concerning none other than the quarry at Bachelors Grove. The hearing was held in 1928 over a dispute regarding the land on which the quarry is housed. Christian Boehm, the owner of the land, had been offered $1,000 per acre for the land as part of the massive development of the forest preserves in the mid- to late 1920s. A series of handwritten notes were included in the Boehm file, in which he contended the price was much too low, considering the improvements he had made on the land—improvements that included a house and a stone quarry. The dispute arose because, at the time of the survey of the land by the Forest Preserve District, the quarry was filled with water, having been out of service for an unspecified number of years. Boehm had moved to Knox, Indiana, and was renting out the Bachelors Grove house to a local resident. A hearing was thus held, calling in witnesses to determine whether, in fact, the water-filled hole was a quarry and, if so, what sort of value it held.

During the testimony, Boehm said he had started the quarry around 1909, which was the year before the land was deeded by the Schmidts to Frederich Boehm, his father, according to the warranty deed drawn up for the sale of the Schmidt land to the Forest Preserve District in 1927. Thus, the quarry did not even exist until at least 1909, so it's impossible that any farmer or horse could have drowned in it decades earlier.

It remains possible that these drownings occurred after the quarry opened, during the later years, when it was often filled with water. Local resident Clarence Fulton told an area reporter that children had drowned in the quarry in his youth. There were horses still used in the area up through the 1930s, so it's possible that a person and their horse or horse-driven cart or trap may have drowned here. If an incident like this did occur after the purchase of the land by the Forest Preserve District, it may very well not have been published in local papers and may instead be sealed in the incident files of the FPD. If any of these drownings occurred before the 1928 hearing, however, it certainly seems likely that any such accident would have been mentioned in the court hearing, during which the FPD attorneys attempted to emphasize the undesirability of the land and the quarry in order to keep the sale price at a minimum. Drownings would have helped their case, presumably. But no such stories were told, though witnesses did make a point of mentioning the "undesirable" location of the quarry land because of its proximity to the cemetery. On the other hand, the locals who testified didn't seem to know much about the land or the area at all. Even Boehm didn't know the name of his own tenants who lived there in his final years of ownership.

The fact remains that at least three witnesses—including two law-enforcement officers—have testified to the apparition of a phantom farmer and a horse and plow or buggy in the vicinity of the quarry pond. In addition, during its first investigation of the cemetery in 1982, the Ghost Research Society had a psychic report that a farmer had drowned in the quarry.

Another odd dimension of this story—possibly connected—came to light in the late winter of 2016, when researcher Wendy Moxley Roe shared with me a strange incident she'd been told regarding this same area of the Grove. Most longtime visitors to the Grove have seen or heard about the "Holy Tree" or "Keebler Tree" at Bachelors Grove: a hollow tree on the creek bank that is home to a statue of the Blessed Virgin Mary. One afternoon, Roe and friends quite accidentally met the woman who had placed the statue there long ago. The woman was riding a horse through the woods surrounding the cemetery and stopped to chat. During this time, the rider shared a curious story. Some years earlier, she had been riding through the creek bed just west of the cemetery when her horse was spooked by something and bolted. The horse was so frightened that it lost its footing and ended up breaking a leg, having to be put down where it fell. Though it must have been a major undertaking to remove this animal from the isolated and difficult-to-access area, no report of the incident turned up in local papers. The incident reports of the Forest Preserve District are sealed for many years to come, so it has been impossible to find any more details about this event, but it's interesting to note that this horse was inexplicably frightened in the same area as the plow horse of local lore. Also interesting is that this rider shared her memories of "Satanic" objects that she had seen tied up on the west fence of the cemetery in the months preceding the incident with her horse.

The Little People

In recent years, I became aware of a most peculiar type of photographic anomaly at Bachelors Grove when I began doing more rigorous investigation of the area and serious genealogical and historical research of its history. At this time, it was not uncommon for me to spend entire days at Bachelors

Grove, investigating, talking with visitors and other researchers, and I discovered that the more time we spent there, the more often images of "little people" would appear in our photographs. The combination of these photographs with the presence of intelligent lights and "orbs," a "lantern man" or "ghost candle" at the cemetery gate and the rumors of treasure buried beneath the cemetery or pond all led me and other researchers to wonder if whatever paranormal or preternatural circumstances make up what folklore calls "fairies" are present here at Bachelors Grove.

The little people have taken many forms, from monochromatic faces of babies and children in the grass to full-color forms of children and small adults, anywhere from a few inches to around a foot and a half tall. A few appear to be soldiers in uniform, possibly from the Civil War or World War I era, or women from the nineteenth century, in long gowns. Some appear to be Native Americans. Others look like hippies or more modern-day young people, with beards and backward baseball caps.

Cherokee Indians tell stories of their own Little People. According to legend, these beings are only about two feet tall but resemble Native Americans. They are said to behave very similarly to the fairies of European lore. At times they can be helpful—doing chores and bringing prosperity—but if you cross them, there is no telling what wrath they will bring upon you. According to the Cherokee, the Little People love music, and it's not uncommon for places they frequent to be "haunted" by "singing" or "chanting," as reported by visitors in their woods. Interestingly for Bachelors Grove folklorists, they will throw spells upon strangers who disturb their peace, causing them to become lost and dazed—a condition that can last literally for the rest of the person's life, evocative of those who say they went home from Bachelors Grove "never quite right again." The Cherokee Little People are particularly angered by people getting drunk. This is compelling, since many "partiers" at Bachelors Grove have been chased off by strange lights, which are believed by some to be manifestations of fairies or elementals.

According to the Cherokee, if a visitor finds something in the woods and wants to take it, he must first ask the Little People to make sure it is not theirs. If this is not done, they will throw stones, sticks or other objects at him as he tries to leave with the object. Interestingly, many visitors to Bachelors Grove have reported being pelted with rocks, sticks or hickory nuts while leaving the Grove. Almost every time, they were taking something with them: sometimes trying to steal a headstone and other times something as simple as taking seeds to grow Bachelors Grove wildflowers at home or taking glass or china fragments from one of the old home sites as souvenirs or to make crafts. I myself experienced this on two occasions. The first time, I had collected some dried tree bark with which I wanted to make some picture frames. The material fit in a brown paper lunch bag. The second time, I had taken a vial of water from the old quarry pond as a souvenir for a friend. It couldn't have been more than an ounce of dirty water. Both times, on the way out, I was pelted with hickory nuts, which hit me as if thrown at the level of my knees. And hard. Needless to say, I have never again removed anything from Bachelors Grove.

One afternoon in the summer of 2013, I snapped a series of photographs of the Big Log outside the cemetery gate, which many clairvoyants believe marks the opening of a portal or interdimensional doorway. When I looked at the photos at home, I saw that there seemed to be a bright spot of light on the log. When I zoomed in, I found what appeared to be a small, luminescent humanoid figure, standing on tiptoe, with some sort of protrusion from its back or shoulders. For obvious reasons, I call the image my "fairy photo."

A Blue Island resident was at the cemetery one summer afternoon in 1998 with his family when he saw what he described as a "fairy" briefly land on his daughter's shoulder and immediately fly off. The figure, he said, was about four inches high, with transparent wings that looked like a dragonfly's. It was definitely humanoid in appearance, but the whole body was of a "luminescent golden color, as if it was made of light instead of substance."

A similar incident occurred during a recent visit by researcher Karl K and local resident Bill Swinford, during which Swinford "saw a fairy fly off Karl" while they were chatting in the cemetery.

In the late 1970s, a scout leader was hiking through the Grove area with his troop along the old Big Foot Trail to the cemetery when they stopped to rest in a clearing not far from the creek. Several large butterflies were flitting around some wildflowers, and the boys were trying to get a closer look at the specimens. The scout leader walked over to his backpack to get out his binoculars and said he saw, perched on the edge of his canteen, a "glowing figure about five inches tall, with deeply veined wings but definite human shape, dart at lightning speed away and disappear." He mentioned nothing to the boys or to the other leaders.

The Little Girl

During a visit to the cemetery by the venerable Ghost Research Society in 1982, a psychic who accompanied the group shared some impressions of the cemetery that have been passed on through oral history and through several books. I would say that this was one of the most famous investigations in Bachelors Grove's history. It was during this visit that this psychic told Dale Kaczmarek that numerous entities in the cemetery are bound there for a certain amount of time. As far as I can find, this was the first mention of the entity of a little girl at Bachelors Grove, as the psychic identified a little girl near the Fulton stone, bound to a man she believed might be her father. She could not move on because she could not leave him behind.

Nicholas Sarlo is the lead investigator of the Shadow Hunters, an Illinois investigative group based in Lake County that is part of a television program called *True Ghost Stories.* He recalled:

> *When we went down there to film an episode for* True Ghost Stories, *we were down by the pond and we had our motion detection system and our REM pod* [a device that detects changes in the immediate EM field] *down there. As we were down there, we felt that we had a connection with a little girl in a white dress. As we were talking to her and asking her questions, the REM pod would light up. We had asked her to also go past the motion detector, and that had also gone off. But what's weird is in my mind, I could see that little girl. And she was wearing a white dress.*

I received a letter from a woman a few years back who had taken a fascinating photograph at Bachelors Grove of a little girl in a blue dress. And numerous visitors have claimed to have a mental image of a little girl in an old-fashioned dress near the Newman stone in the cemetery's southwest quadrant.

In addition to these photographs and psychic images, the sound of a little girl laughing has been experienced by visitors, especially near the Fulton stone and along the banks of the quarry pond.

The Voices

One summer afternoon in 2012, after I had spent an entire Sunday at the Grove talking with visitors, sunset approached. There had been a nearly endless stream of visitors that day, but now a lull had set in, and I said, "It looks like that's the end of visitors for today." I said goodbye to my friends and headed out to the path to walk to my car in the Rubio Woods parking lot. When I left the cemetery and stepped onto the path, a woman's voice spoke directly behind me: "Still more coming!"

I whirled around, assuming that a visitor I hadn't seen had come up behind me, but there was no one there. I looked back into the cemetery and saw my three friends—all male, by the way—chatting across the burial ground at the Fulton stone, so far away I couldn't hear their voices. I continued down the path to where it bends a little, allowing one to see through to the new turnpike road. As I rounded the bend, I came face to face with a group of six women who were celebrating a birthday and visiting haunted locations as a treat. They said to me, "We wanted to get in and out before sundown!" When I told them I had been told of their coming by an unseen presence, they were as spooked as I was.

Very common in the annals of Bachelors Grove experience is the manifestation of audible "voices" to visitors, especially while walking the path to and from the cemetery. Often these voices will have messages to the living—sometimes warning messages, other times simply statements of something docile that is about to happen. More than one visitor has been warned to watch out for booby traps along the path to the creek: wires or fishing line stretched, ankle height, between trees to trip hikers. Law-enforcement officers point out that sometimes practitioners of ritual activities will set these wire traps to keep uninvited guests away from their ritual sites.

Other visitors have been warned about incoming storms or the onset of sundown, the time the preserve closes. One young woman was visiting with her boyfriend several hours before a devastating tornado swept through neighboring Tinley Park. As they lingered at the cemetery gate before getting in their car, they both clearly heard a woman's voice say, "Get home now!" In 1992, a group of friends was gathering up their ghost-hunting equipment when a voice whispered audibly to one of them, "He's waiting for you!" as the last bit of sun dipped over the tree line west of the burying ground. Upon reaching their car, a law-enforcement officer told them to get out earlier next time, that he was about to lock their car in the parking lot.

THE TWO-HEADED MAN

One of the more bizarre and infrequent phenomena reported at Bachelors Grove has been the apparition of a "two-headed man" or "monster."

According to legend, there was a local Bremen couple who gave birth to a terribly deformed infant. At that time, deformed children were believed to have spiritual defects or even diabolical origins, and so in order to avoid the scorn of neighbors, the couple hid the baby in the woods and raised him there, where he grew up and grew older, finally making his home among the trees as an adult. On moonlit nights, they say, you could see the grotesque creature wandering through the trees and among the tombstones of the Grove. Even today, after his death and burial at the Grove, his phantom reportedly walks the grounds he trod in life.

There are some locals who claim that a severely deformed man did live in the area at one time, so the possibility exists that this was an inflation of a very real and unfortunate situation, though the behavior of this figure when seen seems to challenge that possibility.

Sightings of the two-headed man are extremely rare in the annals of Bachelors Grove lore. It would appear that the story originated in the 1990s in an account by W. Haden Blackman in his book *Field Guide to North American Hauntings.* He claimed that the apparition had been seen walking through the cemetery at night. Curiously, like reports of the vanishing house or phantom dogs, Blackman writes that the apparition is typically accompanied by mysterious lights, in this case "dancing blue lights."

According to a report published in the 1989 book *The Uninvited: True Tales of the Unknown,* a couple was driving late one night on the new road and neared the bridge spanning the quarry pond. At that point, they saw what they claimed was a two-headed figure coming up from under the bridge and making its way across the road toward Rubio Woods.

Fellow paranormal researcher Scott Markus interviewed a witness in the 1990s who had been visiting the cemetery when he saw what looked like a disfigured man walking over the surface of the pond. The witness said the man had a large growth or hunch-type protrusion on his shoulder. He had never heard the stories of a two-headed man or monster of the Grove and stated that this was *not* the impression the figure made upon him. It is unclear whether the pond was frozen at the time of the sighting.

Another local resident—now middle aged—remembered a warm April night in the early 1990s when he was in the cemetery near midnight. Sitting in the woods just beyond the tree line, south of the path, the group he was with was waiting to "scare" a group of friends they knew were on their way in. While waiting, they saw a "disabled man with a hunchback" come from the creek area and enter the cemetery, stopping briefly and then walking toward the Pines (an area where there is no other exit). It was a moonlit night, and they could see all the way to the opposite fence, but the man never reappeared.

Looking for instances of two-headed men in folklore as a possible tie-in for the Bachelors Grove stories, I discovered that in English myth the famed Green Man sometimes manifests as a two-headed figure. In such instances, the folklore shows a clear connection to Janus, the Roman god of doorways or gateways. Though it seems unlikely that sightings of a two-headed man at the Grove stretch back to the folklore of the earliest English settlers here, it's an interesting dimension to consider in light of the frequent mention of "caretakers," "guardians," "portals" and "doorways" in the ghost lore of Bachelors Grove. Maybe, just maybe, we are seeing here the influence of the neo-pagan visitors to the Grove in the latter part of the twentieth century.

THE ROBED FIGURES

One of the almost forgotten paranormal manifestations at Bachelors Grove is a phenomenon that was prevalent in the late 1960s and early to mid-1970s: the sighting of hooded or robed figures inside the cemetery or in the surrounding woods. In fact, Phyllis Raybin Emert's 1995 book *The 25 Scariest Places* has an illustration of a black-robed figure in the cemetery. I have come to believe that these sightings were a combination of actual, flesh-and-blood humans who were at the Grove to participate in ritual activities and possibly negative or malevolent entities that were conjured up by these rituals. Strangely, there exist tales of apparitions of robed figures that have appeared to non-sensitives, impressions of robed figures appearing to sensitives and actual robed persons who have been seen in and around the cemetery.

Once again, at least some of the origins of this story were revealed in 1977 when a local woman talked to radio announcer Eddie Schwartz about photographs she took earlier in the year of a "shrouded figure" in the cemetery, which may have led other visitors to "expect" to see similar figures.

On Chicago's WIND Radio in 1977, Richard Crowe shared with Schwartz the fact that a local legend had been circulating of a seven-foot giant at Bachelors Grove. In fact, he revealed:

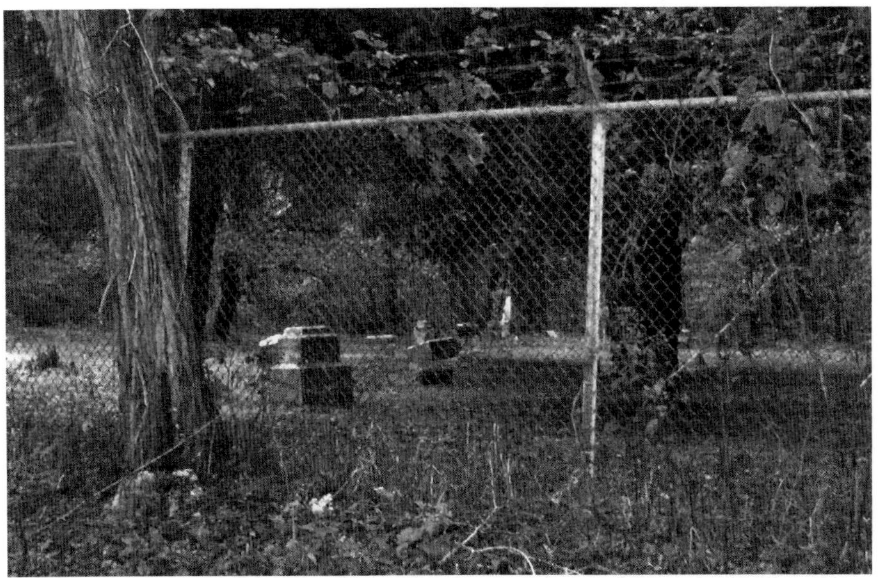

Shirley Sticht captured her sighting of this anomalous image of a figure in a hooded white robe standing next to a tree near the Fulton stone *(far rear, center)*. Many such experiences at Bachelors Grove occur in broad daylight. *Shirley Sticht.*

> *There is a seven-foot guy who frequents the area, quite often, and if it's a full moon he's quite possibly out there tonight. He's a real human being from the Lemont area who dresses in his robes for his different rituals and is seen out there by a number of police who patrol the area as well as unsuspecting teenagers who go out there, who are driving down the road and are confronted by this seven-foot-tall individual in his ceremonial robes.*

But all of these sightings cannot be explained away. Recall the earlier tale told to me by a witness of the magic house, in which two young women saw a literal line of robed figures queued up outside a white farmhouse in the 1970s. When they returned on the path a short time later, both figures and house were gone.

One of the most intriguing incidents involving robed figures took place during a visit to the cemetery in 1982 by Dale Kaczmarek and the Ghost Research Society. Joining the group on this visit was a psychic medium, who told Kaczmarek what she saw and felt about the cemetery, including receiving impressions of a group of people who "tend to wear robes" and of a monk-like figure with a dog's face.

One visitor, Shirley Sticht, actually captured a photograph of a hooded, white-robed figure inside the cemetery, in daylight hours, standing near the Fulton stone. There was no one else in the cemetery at the time.

TEMPERATURE FLUCTUATIONS IN THE ENVIRONMENT AND THE HUMAN BODY

Investigators often point to "cold spots" or temperature dips as evidence of possible anomalous activity. Like battery drain, many believe that the entities present are literally sucking up all the energy or heat in the area as they move through it, creating transient cold spots. Or, they "haunt" a specific place, resulting in static cold spots.

At Bachelors Grove, seemingly countless visitors have experienced cold spots along the path to the cemetery and inside the cemetery itself. Unlike a lot of ostensibly haunted places, where these cold pockets don't register on thermometers, numerous investigators have succeeded in measuring these anomalies at Bachelors Grove.

During one of my own visits to the cemetery, I was able to record temperature drops from the mid-seventies Fahrenheit to the low thirties and from the mid-thirties to zero Fahrenheit on a basic digital thermometer, as well as momentary drops of twenty degrees or more using a thermal scanner or "gun." This suggests that something was passing through the laser and registering at a much lower temperature than the target object (in this case, a tree trunk).

Interestingly, Pat Shenberg, the psychic who visited the Grove with the Ghost Research Society in 1982, was startled by another temperature-related experience. She said that, in her psychic experience, she can tell she is near a grave because it feels warmer to her, but at Bachelors Grove, she did not get this feeling from some of them. Near the Foskett stone in the southwest quadrant, she exclaimed:

> *This is fascinating! This ground here feels somewhat cold, yet whenever you get near a body, heat is much stronger. I'm sure these people have been dead...how many years? Fifty years? That's amazing!*

Dr. Chuck Kennedy visited Bachelors Grove with his wife and another sensitive in the 1990s. He actually measured temperature fluctuations on the outside of his wife's body using a thermal scanner:

> *It was a hot August afternoon. As we walked around, she stopped in her tracks and said something ice cold was on her back. I hit her torso with the thermal gun, and all over her body I was reading in the nineties till I got to her back and I was getting thirty-eight to thirty-nine degrees. She said it was going right through her, so I focused on her abdomen, and it read ninety-five degrees. Then it dropped to the upper eighties then the seventies, sixties, fifties until finally her abdomen was thirty-seven degrees. As she said, "I think it's gone," her abdomen returned to ninety-five degrees.*

Camera and Other Electronics Malfunctions

It would be truly impossible to attempt to document the extent of electronics malfunctioning at the cemetery over these many decades. Battery drain is an epidemic for researchers, who well know that they need to bring dozens of backup or replacement batteries when investigating the Grove. Attempting to conduct sustained, coordinated investigations is an extremely difficult task due to these drains. Generally, researchers believe that these drains occur because of surges in the EM field—or because entities are absorbing the energy from everything around them. But what makes many of these malfunctions different is the fact that they seem to be purposeful; that is, electronics function on their own in order to capture evidence that investigators might otherwise miss.

One of the earliest known occurrences of this was on an afternoon in 1975, when a local man was driving on the turnpike toward the cemetery to take some photographs. As he neared the enclosure, his SX-70 camera began taking pictures on its own. On each of the resulting photos was a white mist, which was a commonly captured image in the earliest days of investigations at the Grove. He sent the camera to Kodak, believing it was broken or flawed, but the company informed him that it was in perfect shape and that the images had been made by something outside the camera.

When Nina Jankowski took her photo of the "Yellow Man" at the Shields stone years ago, she found that her camera had turned itself on and reset itself to a different setting from the one she'd been using (clearly, the ideal setting for capturing her extraordinary image).

The sultry night in 2012 when my colleague and I got lost in the woods, my small digital voice recorder picked up a voice saying, "Here they come!" just as we approached the burying ground from the path. Strangely, when I played back the recording from that night, the recorder had reset itself to play at half speed. It was right after I first bought it, and I thought the batteries that came with it were old and dying down—but no. It was only at this speed that the voice was clearly audible. If it had been set at normal speed, I would never have heard it.

Outside of these odd manipulations of equipment, photographers have captured a huge variety of anomalous images at Bachelors Grove, including figures, shadowy masses, white and blue mists and darting or static balls of white, blue and red light. Our 1980s and '90s experiments verified that an inordinate number of "whities" or "blackies" tended to result from photography at the Grove: photos that were completely overexposed or appeared not exposed at all.

Still other investigators or visitors have claimed that their photographs "changed" over time—that with age, images of people or faces had "developed" in their snapshots or, conversely, that anomalies they once held had later disappeared.

PHYSICAL AND PSYCHOLOGICAL EFFECTS

I always tell people that the first thing to look for in a paranormal investigation is how your body and mind react to the location. Much more common than seeing or hearing ghosts is the interaction of the unseen with our subtler systems and psyches. After all, whatever these phenomena are, they are made of energy.

One of the most extraordinary things I've experienced at Bachelors Grove happened on a beautiful spring day in 2013. The previous winter had brought awful fallout from my involvement with Bachelors Grove. There were rifts between researchers. I had lost friends over the Grove and was struggling to make sense of it all and had almost abandoned my research in frustration. One of these friends and I finally sat down and talked about what had happened. We could not think of any other explanation for the mess than to say that something at the Grove had "gotten between us." When we returned to Bachelors Grove after being away many months, we were standing at the front gate, sunlight beaming down, feeling incredible happiness and contentment, when I sensed something passing forcefully through my body, causing me to literally fall against my friend. The phrase about having the "wind knocked out of me" is what came to mind.

The euphoria we felt before my physical incident is a theme for visitors to Bachelors Grove. Again, this sort of euphoria is a mainstay of Grove experience. So many have reported this feeling over many years, certainly in direct contrast to the "spooky" or "dark" or "depressing" atmosphere one is "supposed" to feel at an abandoned, isolated cemetery. Indeed, this feeling is one of the most peculiar things about the Grove. In fact, some might wonder if it's the result of some kind of very real drug.

In 2001, a geologist, an archaeologist, a chemist and a toxicologist confirmed what ancient history has long suggested: that ancient Greece's famed oracle at Delphi was, in fact, under the influence of petrochemical fumes produced by hidden faults in the oily limestone under the Delphi temple. These fumes, they say, induced the visions that prompted the oracle's pronunciations—and the euphoria or even hypomania with which the oracle spoke. Notably, the researchers found that the oracle was likely under the influence of ethylene—a sweet-smelling gas once used as an anesthetic. In lighter doses, the gas produces feelings of euphoria and carefree ease.

When we observe how happy we are at Bachelors Grove, and how seemingly devoid of care—despite being in a cemetery, among the dead and well informed of the tales of horror in its history—is there some influence from the ground itself? Are we actually getting "high" from vapors produced by faults in the bedrock under Bachelors Grove?

Sometimes, however, the opposite prevails, and it feels obvious that visitors are not welcome. Karl K and Wendy Moxley Roe attest that there are times when the walk into the cemetery—or even simply entering the path—leads one to turn around and walk out again. Karl rarely even goes in the "front" door anymore, down the path. He chooses to walk in from 143rd Street, from the ravine, somehow feeling that, this way, he is less obvious to whatever is there, whatever is waiting for the next person to "mess with."

The "moods" of Bachelors Grove become easier to discern the more one visits—and the more one learns to be aware of them after bad experiences. On a beautiful summer afternoon in 2014, a colleague and I had spent an hour or so at Bachelors Grove Cemetery making some recordings. It was a particularly "happy" day at the Grove, with that familiar undercurrent of contentment absolutely present.

After leaving the cemetery on this particular day, we were headed along the path to the parking lot at Rubio Woods when we passed the entrance to the little footpath off the main path that leads into the woods and the home site there. Just after we cleared it, a forceful wind blew out of the entrance, so loudly that we spun around. We actually saw the tree leaves and branches blowing outward from this one single opening in the tree line. We looked at each other and, intrigued, went back and followed into the woods. Though we saw nothing, we felt as if we were in a trance, quite outside of time, enchanted. When the feeling left after several minutes, we headed back out to the path to find our cars and go home, my colleague to Indiana and me to Chicago. After our goodbyes, I headed to the highway. Though I had enjoyed a great night's sleep and a lazy afternoon, I was overcome with exhaustion. Eventually, with my eyes literally closing, I had to pull off the highway to rest and find coffee before continuing my drive. Later that night, I found that my colleague had been stricken with severe nausea and vomiting on the way to his own home, having to pull over several times in his illness.

Over the years, I have met numerous people who have had similar experiences, including one young man who said he was "never the same" after visiting Bachelors Grove. He felt, even fifteen years later, that half of his natural energy had been "zapped forever, like an appliance that has a power surge and never works right again."

Along with these physical effects, one of the most intriguing aspects of Bachelors Grove is the way it seems to implant the desire to return, often again and again: the "need" to go back, as researcher Karl K succinctly describes it. Karl remembers his first time at Bachelors Grove:

> *The first visit was January 10, 2012, with a friend. It was a weird, amazing feeling walking in. Almost like going to a carnival, exciting… That day, I knew I was coming back. That evening after reviewing the day's photos and seeing what I saw in them…I had much trouble sleeping that night from realizing there is a whole new world going on there of something we know nothing about. I returned the next day alone and went there five of the next nine days.*

Recently, Karl and his research partner, Wendy Moxley Roe, took a survey of visitors to their Bachelors Grove–themed website. They asked, "Did you want to go back?" Overwhelmingly, responders said, they *needed* to go back.

A longtime local researcher from Palos Hills who hosted no fewer than three Bachelors Grove websites estimated that he had visited the Grove some two thousand times over the course of fifteen years.

Another spent years researching the burials at Bachelors Grove from her home—in Florida.

Disorientation is another physical or psychological effect that is hard to explain at Bachelors Grove. Of course, as naturalist Joe Cavataio reminds us, the massive presence of buckthorn is exceptionally good at hiding roads, trails and landmarks from view, even from a short distance away. But there seems to be more to the phenomenon than this. Many who have experienced disorientation in the woods at Bachelors Grove have had the Global Positioning Systems (GPS) on their phones stop working, as they did for my colleague and I in the summer of 2012, despite being in the middle of a populous suburb and right near cell towers. Once back on the main path, functioning returns.

Local resident Bill Swinford, who has walked every inch of these woods, insists that there is one area of the reforestation where it is impossible to not walk in circles. Every time he enters this area, alone or with a group, he ends up lost for a good while.

The creation of animosity between or among investigators or researchers is another strange effect that has been noticed so many times and by so many people as to be considered an anomalous aspect of the Bachelors Grove phenomenon. Timothy Harte is a longtime investigator and one of the creators of the MESA project. MESA (Multi Energy Sensor Array) is a revolutionary custom investigation device composed of the simultaneous feeding into a laptop computer of a variety of environmental sensors, including infrared, visible and ultraviolet light; vibration, electromagnetic fields, static geomagnetic fields and gamma-ray background radiation; and, later, including galvanic skin-response sensors, EKG, EEG and respiration sensors. MESA has been utilized in investigations at Bachelors Grove, where it recorded no light, energy or vibration anomalies, but its designers recorded many experiential incidents over several visits, including seeing mists, lights and even apparitions and feeling physical and emotional changes. Harte made a point of mentioning another aspect of their investigations that stood out to him:

> *With the unusual communications between the MESA team, I would like to put forward a theory that the communication and subsequent misdirection of certain members was in and of itself anomalous and caused great derision within the MESA team.*

As mentioned earlier, I myself experienced this effect numerous times over the years, with other investigators claiming I said things I did not say, did things I did not do or otherwise misinterpreting situations. This was more than just "he said, she said." Over time, it seemed that there was something else at work and that something outside of us was manipulating the situation and was pleased to be the cause of strife, much as Amelia Cotter felt whatever had made her fearful during her visit was enjoying having that effect.

10

THE SECRET OF BACHELORS GROVE

Even after nearly thirty years of studying Bachelors Grove Cemetery and its surrounding area, it's impossible for me to pinpoint the source of what has gained it the title as one of the most haunted places on Earth. This was a one-acre burying ground like ten thousand others that sprang up around myriad settlements during one of the most dynamic times in American history. It's the cemetery by the side of the road that we see in thousands of farm communities across the United States. So, why? Despite a number of unfortunate events occurring here, there was apparently no real massacre, no brutal destruction. No interment of prisoners or mass grave of victims. There was no serial killer or warlock's spell. There are other forest preserves in Cook County with far more documented crimes, deaths and murders than Bachelors Grove.

Skeptics will tell you that it's a typical story of a "haunting": death happens and desecration happens, and the ghost stories begin. Certainly that is a classic sequence of events in many ostensibly haunted places. But these Bachelors Grove stories are far from mere "ghost stories." This place manifests an unheard-of spectrum of truly bizarre activity: images or manifestations of buildings and vehicles; unexplained lights visible day and night and often accompanying the manifestation of other phenomena; countless apparitions or forms—of people and animals—that have been seen walking through the cemetery gates or over the creek into the woods and then vanishing; objects weighing up to five hundred pounds disappearing without a trace and without detection. Visitors falling under "trances" and wandering into the woods to become lost. Physical illness ranging from gastrointestinal distress to fainting, scratches and bites, to psychological effects such as depression or euphoria, unexplained rage, lasting malaise and more. There are also the effects on electronics, from the simple draining of batteries to the manipulation of camera and recording settings, apparently in order to capture specific evidence that would not have been caught if the witnesses were left to their own choices.

One of the circumstances that has come sadly to light with the massive research we've done in the past few years is that there are several whole levels of unidentified graves at Bachelors Grove. First, and obviously, most of the grave markers have been stolen or destroyed. These are the markers on the graves that we knew of, which were documented by students of Bremen High School and Brad Bettenhausen during their years of work on the history of the cemetery. Second are the many graves that may have never been marked: of those whose families could not afford markers, of those who never even had their deaths officially registered and of the dozen or more infants who were interred at family plots but whose deaths were never legally recorded.

I also discovered in the winter of 2016 that numerous vital records exist for patients of Oak Forest Infirmary that include the phrases "Bachelors Grove," "Smith's," "English Bachelors Grove" or "Fulton's," suggesting that deceased patients of the hospital were at least temporarily interred at Bachelors Grove, though some of these records also include the names of other Cook County cemeteries as the place of burial. It seems highly likely that the graves marked as "unsold" were actually set aside for the burial of indigent neighbors or even strangers—not that they were never used. In light of this, it is highly possible that we may never be able to identify these burials by name.

Dale Kaczmarek, perhaps the longest-standing researcher of the Grove, firmly believes that the desecration of the graves remains the most significant factor in the paranormal reality of Bachelors Grove but that the ritual activity in the cemetery and woods beginning in the 1960s introduced something other than mere human spirits into the mix. Indeed, many researchers into the paranormal will affirm that ritual acts as well as violent deaths and even sexual acts—all part of the Grove's unique history—can create energy forms that sometimes remain for a long while and that can affect the living.

It has also been long held that many of the spirits at Bachelors Grove cannot or will not leave for some reason. This contention emerged during that first investigation of the Grove by the Ghost Research Society on May

1, 1982. This was the day that psychic Pat Shenberg picked up on a wide variety of entities at Bachelors Grove and suggested that some of them were stuck there but that many others chose to stay, that it was "a kind of sickness…"—that they *wanted* to stay in a cemetery. She said there was a large gathering of as many as thirty people along the western fence line, including a baker holding a rolling pin and people dressed in 1920s and '30s clothing. She also saw a group of people who "tend to wear robes," including a monk-like figure with a dog's face.

Of course, skeptics have chosen to look for something other than ghosts as the explanation for the extraordinary phenomenon that is Bachelors Grove. More than one researcher has wondered if there is some anomaly in the electromagnetic fields at the Grove, produced by the water of the quarry pond or creek or by the cell towers on the new turnpike road. Could these elements be interfering with the EM field or even causing hallucinations and physical illness? Bachelors Grove researcher Dr. Chuck Kennedy points out that the frequencies produced by the cell towers are not the same frequencies that produce hallucinations. However, it is commonly held by researchers that running water serves as a great conduit for paranormal phenomena, certainly related to the EM field. A disproportionate amount of activity at the Grove seems tied to the creek in some way, and it has been observed that, during high rains, when it flows more freely, activity increases.

The presence of limestone, too, at an ostensibly haunted site sends up the antennae of most modern paranormal researchers, who seem to be constantly looking for limestone as a culprit in reports of the paranormal, believing that its presence can "explain" everything from apparitions to footsteps and cold spots. Therefore, the presence of a quarry at Bachelors Grove has been a consideration for numerous investigators who wonder if the quarry stone is influencing the EM field, "holding on to" energy from the past. This theory is known as the Stone Tape Theory (from the 1970s-era British miniseries called *The Stone Tape*). According to believers in it, the Stone Tape phenomenon can include ghost lights and cold spots; visual, audio and even olfactory apparitions; and more. True, visitors often report euphoric feelings, as well as physical illness such as disorientation, malaise, gastrointestinal issues, hallucinations and other symptoms that can be the result of high EM levels. But how to explain the failure of these skewed levels to register on investigators' equipment at Bachelors Grove? Because they don't.

Along the same thought, despite the fact that they don't live here, are visitors experiencing a "close spiritual affinity" with Bachelors Grove,

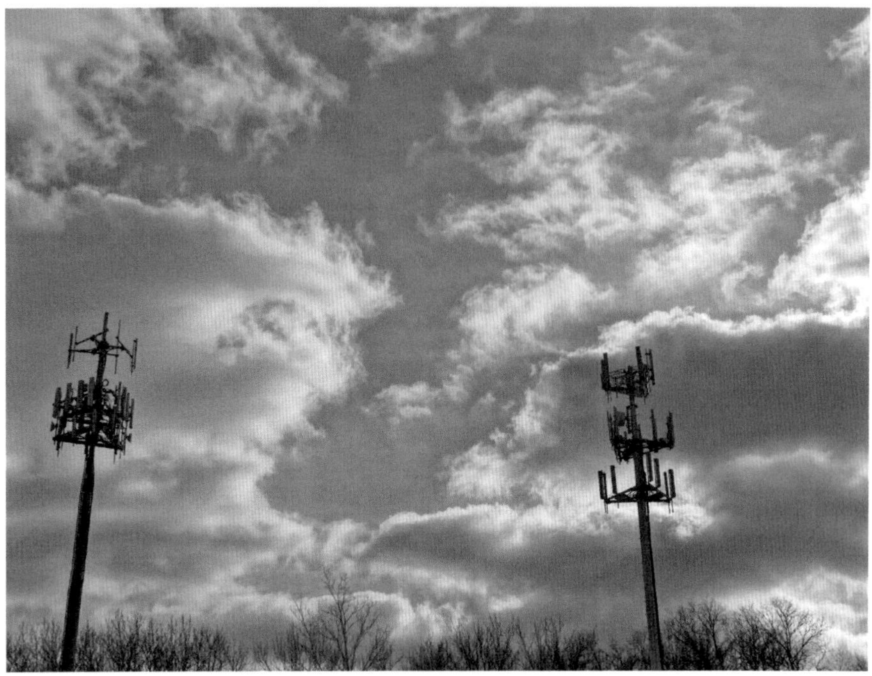

Cell towers stand next to the old turnpike path entrance to Everden Woods, prompting researchers to wonder if they cause disturbances in the EM field, leading to phenomena or hallucinations. *Karl K.*

reminiscent of Jung's theory of his own experience in Ravenna so long ago? When people visit here, do they become opened to an unconscious, shared experience of Bachelors Grove that includes the sights, sounds and smells of eras gone by; of the people, homes, animals and even vehicles that were tied to this land long ago?

This "close spiritual affinity" might be interpreted by scientists quite differently. Timothy Harte reminds us of what parapsychologists call environmental cues, which speaks to our tendency to interpret experiences or even hallucinate based on what we expect to happen. If you bring someone into a location who is expecting or hoping to see phantom houses, dogs, cars and women in white, and that location is somehow physically wired—a la Persinger's Tectonic Strain Theory—to affect brain functioning or even the manifestation of lights or other energies…well, that, as Dr. Persinger has so rigorously researched, is a recipe for a haunting.

Is there a portal or interdimensional doorway here at Bachelors Grove? Some Native Americans tell us that, during the time of encroachment by

Europeans on native lands, their ancestors would sometimes "curse" the land by opening up these portals, ensuring that the white settlers would be constantly tormented by interdimensional visitors coming in and out of these doorways. Visiting clairvoyants tell us that, yes, there is a portal at Bachelors Grove, located right outside the cemetery gate. They tell us the old turnpike road is a "ley line," or spiritual energy line—one of many such lines in the landscape that are said to host rampant paranormal phenomena. Is it a coincidence that these lands were first inhabited by settlers during the very last days of Native American habitation, in 1832, right before the end of the Black Hawk War banished these proud people forever?

Perhaps this reality is evidenced by the many accounts of human-looking figures and animals who have been seen walking through that gate and vanishing and by the "popping" sounds heard and the strange lights seen at the gate. Perhaps this is the cause of lightheadedness and nausea experienced by visitors when they walk through that gate and of the "dancing lights" and "sparks" that are often seen accompanying apparitions. Are these actually the visual and physiological effects of static charges emitted when entities enter or depart through this doorway? Or are they, again, EM effects causing us to hallucinate? The questions, it seems, are endless.

Still, it cannot be denied that there is something at least preternatural at work here, and much older than the settlement of the 1830s, despite the apparent unawareness of it by the European community that briefly lived here. Native American influences or conflicts, the presence of an earlier burial site here, the mysterious origins and vague records of the cemetery, possible EM distortions originating in the bedrock or the water features, the presence of an ancient road fraught with controversy—even if the farmers and families who lived here were too preoccupied with the hard business of life to notice it, did the enigmatic nature of the land show on their faces? Did it show in their lives?

Does it show in ours?

The most confounding thing, to me, about Bachelors Grove is that nowhere before 1930, when everyone left and the isolation and its effects began, did there seem to be any clue to its astonishing paranormality. Combing through court documents of the Forest Preserve District encroachment, the early records of settlers and pioneers, newspaper articles about the burials, nostalgic stories of old-timers who often visited as children, journals of the area, burial records, diaries, local folklore and scores of interviews with those whose families stretch back to its earliest days, there is utterly no mention anywhere of any strangeness, weird activity or cursedness, no mention anywhere of anyone who thought there was anything bad about this place or anything haunted about a cemetery that, by the first moments of vandalism, had already stood for more than a century. Not one.

But there was, indeed, something highly unusual about Bachelors Grove from the beginning: its power of attraction.

Just before this book went to press, researcher Wendy Moxley Roe and I were talking at a wonderful event: the press conference that happened when our friend Dan Melone—an archaeologist—presented to the public the original headstones of one of Chicago's most important settlers, Chief Alexander Robinson, and his family members. Melone had recovered the stones after their disappearance sixty years earlier. As we talked, our conversation of course turned to Bachelors Grove. Wendy asked me if I'd read a book called *Graveyard*, written by the great husband-and-wife paranormal research team of Ed and Lorraine Warren (of *The Conjuring* fame). I said I hadn't, and she told me I absolutely must.

That same day, I purchased the book and read the entire first half, which was a narrative of paranormal encounters at Union Cemetery in Connecticut, known as another of the world's most haunted burying grounds. Knowing little of the place, I was stunned to discover that Union hosts many of the same strange realities as Bachelors Grove: a woman in white in search of her baby; strange deaths and murders that have occurred in its proximity; ritual activity; the sighting of well-dressed men and women who converse with visitors and then disappear, sometimes into areas that are impassable; phantom cars and passengers; ghost lights…the list goes on.

Most extraordinary of all, however, was one similarity in particular: the "hold" of Union Cemetery on many who visit the site. Notably, the book told the tale of a local man who became compelled to take care of the cemetery. With a great job and a wonderful family, he came more and more to choose time in the cemetery, alone, over time living his charmed life with those who loved him. As his attachment progressed, he met one afternoon at Union a young man dressed in deerstalker gear, as if from an earlier century, who spoke as if he was from another time. This meeting only increased his fascination, and he grew obsessed with meeting this person again. Eventually, this young husband and father committed suicide. According to witnesses, a young man in deerstalking clothes was seen during the burial, watching from a hill overlooking the cemetery.

Even in its operative days, Bachelors Grove was a place of refuge from the hard business of pioneer and, later, industrialized life. The youngest of children loved going to Bachelors Grove Cemetery, visiting the pond and

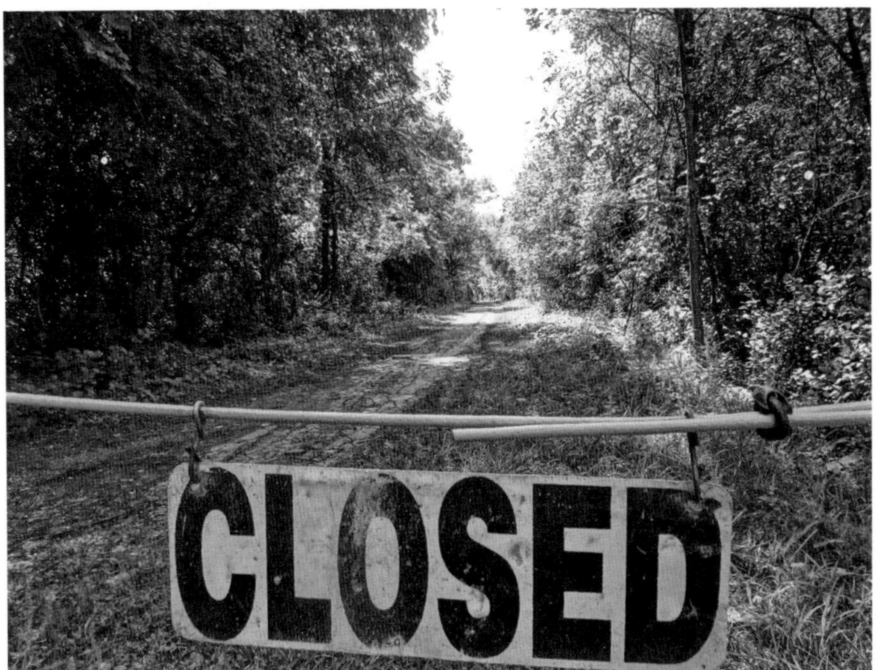

Karl K.

playing in the creek. This strange little place was, for many, a favorite place to be. From the beginning, numerous people were drawn to lovingly tend it, passionately protect it and go to bat for it—to even take precious time away from their families for it. For so many people, Bachelors Grove is still this.

In my thirty years of research, interviewing hundreds of people, the three words most used to describe it have been "peaceful," "beautiful" and "magical."

Until, of course, it gets you where it wants you.

George Lutz, who lived in the famed Amityville house (of *Amityville Horror* fame) on Long Island for less than a month before fleeing with his family, gave a final interview before his death in 2006. In it, he admitted that the events in the notorious house did not unfold as the book and movie portrayed them; they were subtler, more cunning and more purposeful.

Lutz summed up the family's experience with the interesting comment that the house was "charming." When they moved in, he said, he and the family gradually retreated into it from the outside world. George's wife, Kathy, quit classes she was taking. George stopped going to work. Even their children preferred, more and more, to stay home rather than be with friends. The house wanted them there, and whenever they would leave, they felt it pulling, pulling....

Perhaps after everything, this is the only clue we have to the paranormal secret of Bachelors Grove. That for all its negative connotations and all the fallout from its notoriety—and whether the effect is caused by petrochemical fumes, electromagnetic anomalies, evil spirits or the lure of the liminal—one reality shines through the centuries, for better or for worse, and for whatever it may mean.

Bachelors Grove is *charming.*

Step inside.

Appendix A
Notes on the Natural History of Bachelors Grove Cemetery and Environs

Bachelor's Grove Cemetery (BG) is a small cemetery located within the Rubio/Everden Woods preserves in southwestern Cook County. The cemetery, like the forest preserve property immediately surrounding it, is considered highly degraded and of low natural quality. The majority of the woodlands south of 143rd Street is second growth, having been logged and farmed long ago. Invasive shrubs and pole trees (tall, skinny trees stunted by a dense canopy) dominate the landscape. There are few mature native trees, though the cemetery itself was spared of some of its large hardwood trees, such as oaks, as those were considered visually pleasing to cemetery visitors and provided shade on hot days. Prominent invasive plant species include common buckthorn (*Rhamnus cathartica*), wild grape (*Vitis* spp.) and garlic mustard (*Alliaria petiolata*), as well as a host of others.

The overabundance of invasive woody shrubs and trees results in a very closed-in, claustrophobic experience. Visitors who decide to veer off the path that leads to the Grove from 143rd Street may find themselves pushing their way through a nearly impenetrable wall of thorny, woody invasive plants. Large, native trees such as oaks take long to grow and mature, and invasive species can easily rush in and populate an open area much quicker, eventually killing oak saplings as they suffocate in the invasive understory. Within the Grove, much restoration has taken place recently that would allow for the successful reproduction of native hardwood trees. However, the cemetery succumbs to large groups of visitors, many of whom have carelessly damaged or destroyed much of the native plant life. A professionally planned restoration plan and regular volunteer-driven workdays would, over time, transform the surrounding woodlands into a healthier ecosystem that would more accurately resemble a pre-settlement landscape as well as attract native wildlife and improve the overall balance of the preserve. Restorative activities would include the removal of buckthorn, garlic mustard and other invasive species; the application of herbicide to stumps; prescribed burns; and supporting young or stunted native trees such as oaks and hickories by caging them from deer. A restored woodland surrounding Bachelors Grove could boast beautiful ephemeral wildflowers such as bloodroot and *Trillium* and potentially many others.

Here are some additional notes on buckthorn. Common buckthorn is native to Eurasia. It was first introduced to the United States during the late eighteenth or early nineteenth century for its use as an ornamental plant. Its specific name, *cathartica*, is a reference to its fruit: small, deep red or black berries that are very cathartic (www.henriettes-herb.com/eclectic/kings/rhamnus-cath.html). The berries ripen during the fall and are eaten by many types of birds. As the birds pass the seeds in their droppings, they land on the ground—along with a convenient supply of fertilizer—and quickly re-colonize elsewhere. The plant itself—leaves, stems, etcetera—is toxic; therefore, most deer will avoid eating it unless they are desperate. Common buckthorn grows in dense stands and out-competes native trees and plants. It allows little to no light to reach the woodland floor, eliminating the possibility of native grasses and wildflowers in most cases. In addition, it alters the chemical makeup of the underlying soil through an allelopathic chemical in its roots and has been known to negatively impact the development of larval amphibians (www.bioone.org/doi/abs/10.1670/12-066). All of these symptoms of the spread of common buckthorn are evident in the woods surrounding Bachelors Grove. Buckthorn can be identified by its scraggly stems, which grow singly or often in multiple "clumps." Where there is one, there are usually many more, as they grow in thickets and create monocultures. They are easiest to identify in early spring and late fall, since they are one of the first plants to produce leaves and one of the last to drop those leaves (www.ecolandscaping.org/12/invasive-plants/common-buckthorn-an-exotic-invasive-plant-fact-sheet/, http://removebadplants.com/buckthorn/).

Perhaps more relevant at Bachelors Grove/Rubio Woods than at other preserves is the idea that buckthorn has the potential to increase incidents of crime (http://removebadplants.com/buckthorn/). Buckthorn creates barriers beyond which little to nothing can be seen. Illegal activities are nothing new to the Grove, and the abundance of buckthorn might facilitate fly dumping, vandalism, gang activity (including spray-painting) or ritualistic activities that can cause harm to both humans and nature. Buckthorn is most evident along the path that leads to the Grove from 143rd Street.

A persistent ground-cover plant that many regret ever planting in the first place is lesser periwinkle (*Vina minor*). Extremely common in gardens and graveyards, this plant consists of green, waxy-looking, oval-shaped leaves and small, beautiful lavender flowers that bloom from spring to mid- or late summer. Though attractive, this species grows in clonal colonies (interlinked through roots) to create dense mats in which little else can grow. Despite recent restoration in the cemetery, which resulted in the destruction of many other plants, lesser periwinkle lives on and probably will for a very long time.

Here are a few notes on other species seen either in person or through YouTube video tours and older photos. Goldenrod (*Solidago altissima/canadensis*) is a native and sometimes invasive wildflower common in the open parts of both Bachelors Grove and the path that leads to it; it attracts all sorts of butterflies and insects. Common milkweed (*Asclepias syriaca*) is another common native, famous for hosting the larval form of the monarch butterfly (*Danaus plexippus*). Queen Anne's Lace, or wild carrot (*Daucus carota*), is an invasive tall plant with tiny white flowers. It can be seen along the path, where it savors the sun. Wild parsnip (*Pastinaca sativa*) is a commonly occurring invasive that is often seen in old fields or roadsides. It was encountered along the path to the Grove. It is of some importance due to its toxic nature; if the plant's juices end up on your skin (from breakage, etcetera) and the sky is sunny, the sun activates chemicals that cause phytophotodermititis, a condition that includes red sores and blisters on the skin. The sensation has been likened to the rash caused by poison ivy (*Toxicodendron radicans*), but the resulting redness/discoloration can remain on the skin for up to two years (William L. Brenneman, *50 Wild Plants Everyone Should Know*. N.p.: 2010, AuthorHouse, 38). It's important to learn how to identify the flowers and leaves of wild parsnip before you veer off the path. Poison ivy has also been seen, in large amounts, growing as vines on trees along the path that leads to Bachelors Grove. In short, it is not recommended that persons veer off the path.

The trees within the perimeter of Bachelors Grove tell a great story of how the cemetery was planned and considered long ago. In it are both trees that are native and those that are nonnative (cultivated by man)—the latter maintained as aesthetic components and sources of shade. Examples of native trees include oak, hickory, black walnut and black cherry. Mulberry and white cedar constitute two of the more prominent nonnative species.

Oaks (*Quercus* spp.) are among the most coveted and mighty trees in the Illinois landscape. Long appreciated for their valuable timber, oaks have experienced a decline since European settlers arrived and exploited them for their benefit. Oak wood is very versatile and was (and still is) used in frame home construction, furniture, barrels and other items. Ecologically, oaks are considered keystone species (R.T. Paine, "A Conversation on Refining the Concept of Keystone Species." *Conservation Biology* 9, no. 4 (1995): 962–64. doi:10.1046/j.1523-). They have a profound influence on the shaping of their respective biomes. Often associated with wisdom and strength, oaks are one of the more symbolic organisms one might find in a woodland ecosystem. They are hardy, long-lived and highly resistant to the fires that helped shape their habitat before fires were suppressed by man long ago (restorationists now consider fire one of the most useful tools in bringing damaged habitat back to life). It is likely that the oaks in the Grove either predate the cemetery or were planted early in the life of the cemetery.

Along with oaks, hickories (*Carya* spp.) are one of the more defining hardwood trees in the area's woodlands. Like oaks, their wood is used for the construction of a multitude of items. Hickory trees produce fruits that contain nuts, some of which are edible (http://waynesword.palomar.edu/ecoph8.htm). These nuts can be found littering the cemetery, sometimes embedded in the ground after being stepped on. Squirrels and chipmunks love them. There are large examples of hickory in Bachelors Grove (exact species unknown), and they, like the oaks, have persisted for a long time, through—and sometimes despite—all of the tragedies inflicted on the cemetery by vandals.

Black cherry (*Prunus serotina*) and black walnut (*Juglans nigra*) are two other native species found in Bachelors Grove. Both black cherry and black walnut are considered pioneer species—species that are first to colonize previously disrupted ecosystems (Leslie A. Duram, *Encyclopedia of Organic, Sustainable, and Local Food*. N.p.: ABC-CLIO, 2010, 48). It is likely that these two species prosper here due to the open, biologically disturbed nature of the cemetery. They may have developed naturally here, or they may have been transplanted/cultivated at one time. They love sunlight, and they both produce fruit that attracts wildlife, cherries and walnuts, respectively.

As far as I can tell, the mulberry trees present in the Grove are white mulberry (*Morus alba*), but they could possibly be another related species. They are native to Asia and are considered naturalized in the United

States (naturalized differs from invasive, in that a naturalized species cannot reproduce independently and spread unabated. It only exists where it is due to continued influx from somewhere else [Warren L. Wagner, Derral R. Herbst and Sy H. Sohmer. *Manual of the Flowering Plants of Hawai`i*, Revised Edition, Honolulu, HI: Bishop Museum Press, 1999]). Mulberry trees are relatively short-lived and are widely cultivated, often in cemeteries (I have personally seen examples in other older cemeteries such as Union Ridge Cemetery in Chicago). They produce edible, sweet berries in summer. Oftentimes, the fallen fruit ferments on the ground and, in the heat of the day, attracts flies and bees.

Perhaps the most identifiable trees in Bachelors Grove are the large white cedars (*Thuja occidentalis*) just past the front gate. White cedars are sometimes known as the eastern arborvitae, meaning "tree of life" in Latin (www.conifers.org/cu/Thuja_occidentalis.php). In reality, these are not cedars at all but rather in the cypress family. As an evergreen conifer, it is green year-round. The white cedars really stick out in the Grove during the winter months, as they are the only evergreens in the area (view the cemetery on Google maps; you'll see what I mean). Though the white cedar's range extends south to the Chicago area from its core range in Canada, the specimens at BG are almost certainly cultivated, probably in the early twentieth century. They are an extremely popular choice for cemeteries, parks and yards (www.illinoiswildflowers.info/trees/plants/white_cedar.html). These are long-lived trees; assuming the ones in Bachelors Grove are "only" about a century old, they could live another seven to eight hundred years, if conditions are favorable. Interestingly enough, the two large white cedars near the front gate of the cemetery are clearly discernable in a 1939 aerial photo on www.historicaerials.com/—the only two trees that can be identified with a great deal of certainty.

In and around Bachelors Grove, there are numerous ash trees (*Fraxinus* spp.) that have been ravaged by the invasive emerald ash borer (*Agrilis planipennis*), a green beetle native to eastern Asia. The beetle's larvae lives and feeds within the phloem, cambium and outer xylem layers of a tree—thin layers between the bark and the heartwood. This disrupts the transfer of water and nutrients; in most cases, an afflicted ash tree dies within a few years. Green ash trees (*Fraxinus pennsylvanica*) alone make up 5.5 percent of the Chicago region's 157,142,000 trees (www.itreetools.org/resources/reports/Chicago_Region_rb_nrs84.pdf). Afflicted ash trees are typically removed by the respective county, but relatively little attention has been given to those in the Rubio Woods preserves. Therefore, an increased number of dead and dying trees around Bachelors Grove has resulted in yet another "haunted" aspect of the area.

One of the very few upsides to the emerald ash borer explosion has been the accompanying increase in various woodpecker species. Woodpeckers, which search for insect larvae in dead wood, have enjoyed a bounty of food over the last decade in the Chicago region. Woodpeckers can be heard rapping on trees throughout Rubio Woods, doing their part to both help eliminate the larvae and create an uneasy, spooky sound to those, particularly city-dwellers, unfamiliar with the habits of such birds.

Of course, many other species of birds are found in Rubio Woods. A few of the birds I have personally observed have been European starlings (*Sturnus vulgaris*), American robins (*Turdus migratorius*), various sparrows (family *Passeridae*), northern cardinals (*Cardinalis cardinalis*), blue jays (*Cyanocitta cristata*), mourning doves (*Zenaida macroura*), black-capped chickadees (*Poecile atricapillus*), white-breasted nuthatches (*Sitta carolinensis*), American goldfinches (*Spinus tristis*), Cooper's hawks (*Accipiter cooperii*), red-tailed hawks (*Buteo jamaicensis*), various ducks (family *Anatidea*), owls (Order *Strigiformes*) and American crows (*Corvus brachyrhynchos*). (The latter two, again, can contribute to the eeriness of the woods at the right times.) A more thorough bird survey of the Grove and Rubio Woods would undoubtedly result in a longer list.

Herpetofauna (reptiles and amphibians) of Bachelors Grove and the surrounding woods is limited in variety, though a few species are common to abundant locally. Bullfrogs (*Lithobates catebeianus*) are the frogs often seen and heard in the quarry pond adjacent to the cemetery. Bullfrogs are the largest species of frog native to the Chicago region and one of the largest, if not the largest, in the United States. They are extremely adaptable and are highly tolerant of a relatively high degree of pollution and disturbance. They are known to be aggressive feeders, eagerly consuming prey ranging from small insects and fish to other bullfrogs, small rodents and even birds that come to the water for a drink. Bullfrogs in the region typically breed during late spring to midsummer, during which time the males' distinctive "rum… rum…rum" bellows can be heard. I have found juvenile bullfrogs along Tinley Creek, which flows alongside Bachelors Grove and through Rubio Woods. American toads (*Anaxyrus americanus*) are the common toad species found in and around the Grove. Toads are much less reliant on water than the bullfrogs; they head to ponds in the spring to breed and lay their eggs, but once done, they head back into the woods, where they live a secretive lifestyle. They spend most of their time hiding under logs and leaf litter, emerging at night or during rain events to hunt insects. The toad tadpoles metamorphose during the summer, leaving the water and remaining hidden as best as possible. I presume that the resident bullfrogs eat a significant number of young toads during the summer, while the toadlets are exposed and vulnerable.

Notes on toads: contrary to old wives' tales, American toads will not give you warts if you pick them up—not even Grove toads! They will, however, urinate on your hands in the hopes that they will be released.

I am uncertain whether or not there are salamanders living near Bachelors Grove, though they are found in surrounding preserves, including some areas north of 143rd Street. A more thorough survey of the area is needed.

Snakes can be found in and around Bachelors Grove, mostly Chicago garter snakes (*Thamnophis sirtalis semifasciatus*). The Chicago garter snake is a subspecies of the common garter snake, and it differs from many other common garter snakes by possessing a slightly different pattern. Averaging between one and two feet in length, Chicago garter snakes are abundant and extremely adaptable, though they prefer open woodlands, woodland edges, savannahs and sometimes open fields or prairies. Much of Rubio Woods is closed canopy, which creates challenges for the garter snakes, since a shaded woodland offers little to no sunlight for the snakes to bask in. The Grove is an exception, as it features a more open canopy. Bachelors Grove's proximity to the quarry pond is also advantageous for the garter snakes, as they will hunt and eat small bullfrogs, bullfrog tadpoles, leeches, worms and other organisms associated with a wet or watery environment. The Chicago garter snake, like all garter snakes, is completely innocuous to humans and poses no threat to the hiker or cemetery visitor. When approached, they will either remain still to avoid detection or slither away very quickly. Only when cornered or handled might the garter snake defend itself by writhing wildly, squirting an acrid-smelling musk or biting. A bite from a garter snake causes more harm to the garter snake than it does to the handler—a reason these animals should be viewed from a distance and allowed to go on their way without harassment.

A close second in abundance is probably the midland brown snake (*Storeria dekayi wrightorum*). Also known as the Dekay's brown snake or just Dekay's snake, this tiny snake, which rarely grows longer than twelve inches in length, can be found throughout Rubio Woods and in and around the Grove. The midland brown snake is mostly fossorial, which means underground-dwelling, though it can often be seen crawling about along the forest floor, particularly during the spring and fall. It is a light brown to grey snake that has an interesting diet: slugs and snails, mainly, along with the occasional small worm. Like the garter snake with which it shares its range, it is a harmless, nonvenomous and shy snake that tries all it can to avoid people. When handled, it is much less likely to bite than the garter snake, but it nevertheless will not hesitate to coat your hands in a very offensive-smelling musk meant to deter predators.

An interesting variety of mammals inhabit Rubio Woods and Bachelors Grove. They range from tiny mice, voles and shrews to bats and from the all-too-familiar opossums, skunks and raccoons to deer and coyotes. Mice, voles and shrews, all members of the rodent family, are important members of the ecological balance of the woods and are readily stalked by hawks, owls and coyotes. Opossums (*Didelphis virginiana*) are North America's sole representative of the marsupial family. They are extremely unspecialized and can be found anywhere from pristine nature to alley dumpsters in downtown Chicago. Though often regarded as a pest, they actually play an important role as an omnivore, eating both plant and animal material. They are solitary as adults and mostly nocturnal. They have an interesting strategy for protecting themselves from predators: "playing possum." When approached by a dog or other predator, they will collapse and lie on the ground with their mouths open. This deters a lot of predators, which prefer not to eat something already dead. Shortly after the predator leaves the scene, the opossum will revive itself and go on its way. Unfortunately, opossums haven't grasped the concept of automobiles, and playing dead in front of an approaching vehicle most often does not end well. It is not uncommon to see road-killed opossums along 143rd Street at Bachelors Grove, or any road for that matter.

The raccoon (*Procyon lotor*) is similar to the opossum in that it is an unspecialized, cat-sized, omnivorous, nocturnal mammal. But the raccoon does engage in social behavior to a somewhat higher degree than the opossums do. The raccoon is a faster runner and, as a result, is seen more alive than dead along roads. It is a more efficient hunter than the opossum and probably better utilizes the pond and creek for hunting for food. If it can catch a frog, toad or crayfish, it will eat it.

Skunks (*Mephitis mephitis*) are very common around Bachelors Grove. Best known for their infamous odor, they lumber about in woods and urban areas with a certain cockiness that can only be attributed to their mode of defense. A skunk's spray can be smelled for several square miles under the right conditions, much to the disgust of humankind. Like opossums and raccoons, skunks are nocturnal and omnivorous.

The prevalence of bats in and around Bachelors Grove can only bode well for those who expect a haunted experience. Though it is unclear which species of bats are found near the Grove (a survey would help), there are seven species of bats in the Chicago area. The largest of the seven, the big brown bat (*Eptesicus fuscus*), usually weighs about three-quarters of an ounce. This tells you that any bat seen is going to be small. But, though small, they are extremely efficient as a natural form of pest control. Bats eat mosquitoes, among other insects, reducing the likelihood that you will be bitten by the potentially disease-spreading bugs. Still, most people have a fear of bats, and those fears usually stem from two misconceptions: that bats will fly into your hair; and that bats will give you rabies. First, bats are extraordinarily good flyers. Watch as a colony of bats skillfully flies about without contacting each other. This is due to their use of echolocation—"bio-sonar" that aids them in their hunting and communication. Flying into someone's hair does not benefit a bat in any way, shape or form, so people shouldn't worry about that happening. The second fear people have isn't completely unwarranted. In the United States, between 1997 and 2006, there were a reported nineteen cases of naturally acquired rabies; seventeen were associated with bats. However, rabies overall is extremely rare in the United States, with only one or two cases per year on average (www.cdc.gov/rabies/bats/education/). Almost all instances of bat-related rabies were the result of intentional human-bat interactions (such as someone removing a bat from a home). Suffice it to say, it is completely safe to be in the presence of bats, as long as they are respected. Since bats are nocturnal and mostly seen around dusk, most visitors will probably not witness them at the Grove. But pay attention to the sky later in the afternoon or early evening before dark, and you may witness the flight of one or more of these amazing mammals. The quarry pond is a mosquito factory, so perhaps focusing in that direction could yield a sighting.

An additional note on bats: the phrase "blind as a bat" is a misnomer. It isn't fully clear how that phrase came to be, as bats can see quite well. It could be, perhaps, because a bat's echolocation and hearing are better developed than its vision, but that shouldn't negate the fact that they can in fact see well enough to get by (www.todayifoundout.com/index.php/2011/02/bats-are-not-blind/).

Aside from squirrels, probably the most commonly seen mammal in and around BG is the white-tailed deer (*Odocoileus virginianus*). White-tailed deer are one of the most widespread large mammals in the Western Hemisphere, ranging from northern Alaska south to South America. They can be found in both wooded and open landscapes. In high densities, deer can cause serious damage to the ecosystem (www.inhs.illinois.edu/resources/inhsreports/may-jun99/deer/). Such a problem exists in the Chicago suburbs, including Midlothian and Rubio Woods. As human development steadily replaces deer habitat, the deer become concentrated in smaller preserves with well-defined boundaries. The deer eat copious amounts of plant matter (but again, usually not buckthorn) and can ravage an ecosystem of its biomass in short order. Over time, their actions can completely reshape the forest structure, leaving the forest floor bare and vulnerable to succession by invasive pioneer plant species. A large deer population can quickly eliminate an entire season's worth of acorns, allowing no chance for the mighty oaks to witness their progeny take hold and begin the next generation. Plans to manage the deer populations in the Chicago area have been met with stern opposition by many citizens (www.chicagotribune.com/lifestyles/pets/ct-pets-deer-0123-20150123-story.html). Though deer are beautiful and graceful animals, culling is the only way to maintain healthy populations, and it reduces the likelihood of ecological destruction, inbreeding and vehicular-related deer strike.

A summary of the mammals of Bachelors Grove/Rubio Woods would not be complete without the inclusion of the coyote (*Canis latrans*). The region's premier land predator, the coyote is much like a ghost itself around the Grove—elusive and enchanting. The coyote is enjoying a resurgence in the Chicago area after being extirpated long ago. At one time, it was joined by other large land predators in the region: bobcats, wolves and black bears. It is now the sole representative of a group of often-maligned animals that actually perform priceless ecological services to humans. Coyotes in and around the Grove are primarily hunters of small game—rodents and other small mammals, birds, snakes, frogs and even young or sick deer constitute its natural diet. However, as opportunistic feeders, they will even ransack human garbage for food scraps and occasionally make off with an outdoor cat or even a small dog. Coyotes are not usually a threat to humans, though it would be wise to avoid approaching one. At Bachelors Grove as elsewhere, coyotes are often heard more than they are seen, their classic whines, yelps and howls carrying across the landscape like disembodied voices from afar.

—Joe Cavataio

Appendix B.

Current Known Burials at Bachelors Grove Cemetery

The burials at Bachelors Grove Cemetery are perhaps the greatest of its mysteries.

Years of vandalism, destruction and neglect have literally wiped away what little evidence used to stand out proudly on its headstones. Due to the efforts of a few over the years, pieces of information have managed to survive and be passed on for future generations to try to piece together and sort out. One of the problems with this, however, is that there are so many small pieces, and some "official" records were educated guesses trying to connect the dots, which in the end turned out to be incorrect. In turn, these mistakes have been spread across Internet genealogy sites and into family trees and historical databases.

Described here is the picture of Bachelors Grove Cemetery that we have been able to put together so far, keeping in mind that this effort has been a major focus in our lives for several years. We have been exhaustively dissecting each lot to see what we could really discover about them, using funeral home records, vital records, obituaries, family histories, newspaper articles and more. It's an ongoing process and far from complete. But we've found records for people who weren't known to be here before. And we've found that others formerly believed interred here are not.

Each person in this list, then, has some form of evidence listing their actual burial place as Bachelors Grove Cemetery. In no way would we consider it a complete list, as it probably never will be. With no official burial records found to date and only business transactions said to have been recorded on a plot map by trustees or caretakers, it is hard to even guess at how many could possibly be buried within.

There are a dozen or more infants and children with no known death and/or burial records who were born to women who were eventually interred at Bachelors Grove or who had family members interred at the Grove at the time of the children's deaths. We know of them from family records, though no county, state or church records have yet been found to verify their deaths. There are strong odds that these children are also interred at Bachelors Grove, but in good faith we cannot include them on this list.

We have also found numerous death/burial records for patients who died at Oak Forest Infirmary, which lists "Bachelors Grove," "Everdens," "Fulton's" or "English Bachelors Grove" on the burial records. Some of these records also include references to other cemeteries. We do not know at this time if these individuals were interred at Bachelors Grove Cemetery (either temporarily or permanently) or if there were plans to inter them thusly. We do not know at this time if any of these individuals were actually interred at Bachelors Grove, but there is strong evidence to suggest that at least some of them were and are.

Whether there were hospital dead interred here or not, it now seems clear that peripheral sections of the cemetery were set aside for indigents' or paupers' graves. As was common in Chicago-area cemeteries, there may have been a cemetery ordinance against placing headstones on these free graves, even if family existed and had money to purchase them.

Bachelors Grove was one of the first burial places for local settlers and farmers. In a time before elaborate funeral and burial practices became popular, this small cemetery was started when a cedar tree or wooden cross was the only thing that marked a burial site. When other cemeteries opened up in the area, Bachelors Grove then became the place for locals to economically bury relatives in a no-frills, no-thrills way, as there was not much overhead cost for staff and upkeep.

We believe firmly that there are some buried within whose graves—and identities—time has totally erased. We also believe this cemetery is older than current burial records state.

We have spent many hours in historical societies and archives, as well as researching online resources and sifting through records trying to put together the most accurate burial list we can. (Entries marked with two asterisks indicate burials found by us.) It has been a "labor of love," as we so often call it. It has been, at times, overwhelmingly confusing and frustrating, but ultimately exhilarating, as we have come to love and care for these people just as if they were family to us.

We strive to bring dignity and respect to the dead of Bachelors Grove that the past years have taken away. We steadfastly forge forward, honoring these brave and wonderful people by continuing our research so they will always be remembered.

—Wendy Moxley Roe
Harwood Heights, Illinois

—Ursula Bielski
Chicago, Illinois

Lots 1–3
Multiple unknown burials. Marked as unsold.**

Lot 4
Emma Schmidt (October 1, 1885–December 8, 1964)

Lot 5
Louis Buch (Bock) (1837–1888)
Johanna Buch (Bock) (?–?)
John Bock (1798–c. 1895) and possibly his widow, name unknown**

Lot 6
August Aschenbach (1827?–September 9, 1895)
Margaret Aschenbach (née Kirk) (1843–August 30, 1923)
August Aschenbach Jr. (c. 1883–November 17, 1910)

Lot 7
Louise Frundle (née Aschenbach) (December 14, 1877–February 9, 1931)
James Frundle (March 18, 1918–July 12, 1942)
Howard Frundle (November 6, 1914–March 26, 1963)**
William H. Frundle (July 30, 1898–February 22, 1955)

Lots 8–14
Multiple unknown burials. Marked as unsold.**

Lot 15
John Fulton Jr. (December 8, 1838–January 3, 1922)
Hulda Fulton (née Turney) (July 2, 1849–February 3, 1919)
Emma Fulton (August 26, 1867–September 10, 1867)
Johnnie B. Fulton (December 4, 1882–February 28, 1891)
Frank J. Fulton (September 21, 1874–May 22, 1906)
Luella Rogers (née Fulton) (c. 1879–January 23, 1937)
Daniel Rogers (August 29, 1862–September 16, 1923)
Marci May Fulton (1914–1914)

Lot 16
William Hamilton (1807–?)
John Hamilton (July 27, 1842–December 28, 1925)
Alma G. Hamilton (née Lucas) (June 9, 1857–June 7, 1954)
Margaret Roberson (née Hamilton) (February 7, 1847–May 29, 1922)
John P. Roberson (December 31, 1848–October 16, 1917)
Mary Jane Briggs (née Hamilton) (?–?)

Lot 17
William H. Shields (November 8, 1839–June 3, 1922)
Sarah Shields (née Moss) (December 10, 1841–December 22, 1924)
James H. Shields (April 18, 1865–June 1, 1918)
Frank Shields (August, 27 1873–November 30, 1938)
Thomas W. Shields (September 3, 1863–December 11, 1946)
Anna Shields (March 14, 1871–March 24, 1952)
Charles Baxter Shields (June 20, 1868–November 26, 1955)
Elizabeth Shields (April 8, 1881–May 17, 1959)
Robert E. Shields (December 12, 1917–October 10, 1989)
George Turley B: (?–c. 1852)

Lot 18
Lorena Ramsdell (1801–1873)
Carl August Panknin (September 4, 1874–July 5, 1939)

Lot 19
Edna Wright Hardy Sanderson (November 20, 1829–August 30, 1907)

Lot 20
Empty. Marked as unsold.

Lot 21
Multiple unknown burials. Marked as unsold.**

Lot 22
Jacob Deck (April 30, 1840–June 30, 1915)
Mary Deck (née Daslin) (1841–January 20, 1921)
Jennie Niklas (née Deck) (1871–July 22, 1921)
Joseph Niklas (March 16, 1875–July 22, 1921)
Bernard Franklin Deck (June 24, 1875–1949)

Lot 23
David Hulett (September 6, 1830–January 20, 1893)
Ida E. Hulett (?–October 8, 1889)
Whittemore Hulett (?–1862)

Lot 24
Heinrich Christian Gottfried Frederich (Frederich) Schmidt (March 31, 1808–January 16, 1899)**
Ilse Dorothea Regine Eleonore (Dorothea) Schmidt (née Hamell) (August 12, 1813–November 14, 1903)**

Lot 25
Several members of the Mark Crandall family were buried here until June 6, 1892, when they were reinterred at Mount Greenwood Cemetery in Chicago.

Lot 26
Jane McMurray (née Fulton) (February 18, 1831–December 19, 1911)
Robert McMurray (January 4, 1831–May 29, 1909)
Lots 27–34
Multiple unknown burials. Marked as unsold.**

Lot 35
Alvin Frank Rick (March 20, 1924–June 17, 1953)**
Marjorie Rick (September 7, 1921–October 6, 1928)**

Lot 36
Ezra Snow Warren (October 1804–November 28, 1883)
Susan Warren (née Lamson) (1812–August 23, 1880)
Richard Martin Warren (October 29, 1844–March 3, 1875)
Stephen Warren (1846–?)
Mark Ichabod Warren (1853–June 29, 1904)
Amezetta Warren (née Curtis) (March 1862–1901)
Several third-generation Warren infants and children are almost certainly also interred here.**

Lot 37
Unknown burials. Plat map notations list Robert Patrick as owner of this lot. No known burials at this time.

Lot 38
West half of lot:
Alphonse Carley (1822–1861)
Rosa C. Kollman (?–1866)

East half of lot:
Martha Weber (?–1856)
Catherine Weber (?–1856)

Lot 39
Hamilton Fulton (1822–1876)
Mary Jane Fulton (?–1896)
Margaret Law (née Fulton) (May 3, 1860–September 6, 1922)**
John Law (October 17, 1857–August 15, 1938)**

Lot 40
Fred Borman (probably George Frederick Borman) (?–1886)

Lot 41
John Rippet (August 20, 1833–February 28, 1907)
Mary Eliza Rippet (née Aston) (April 30, 1840–September 27, 1907)

James Rippet (1859–October 26, 1920)**
Robert Aston (?–1861)

Lot 42
Unknown burials. Plat map notations list E. Daniels as owner of this lot.

Lot 43
North half of lot:
Delaney Ann McKee (née Hulett) (September 18, 1855–April 16, 1920)
James W. McKee (October 8, 1845–July 21, 1911)

South half of lot:
Richard Edmund Moss (March 6, 1859–March 9, 1934)
Maria Moss (née Farquharson) (December 29, 1854–October 19, 1918)
Hazel Moss (died October 21, 1900, at nineteen months old)
Laura McGhee (née Moss) (January 8, 1887–November 17, 1965)
Robert McGhee (September 10, 1876–July 31, 1939)

Lot 44
Walter Patrick (February 7, 1820–March 18, 1887)
Hannah A. Patrick (née Cowan) (1818–August 1, 1871)
Naomi Elizabeth Patrick (February 1839–January 1, 1880)
Clara B. Patrick (September 28, 1855–January 7, 1862)
Lillie E. Patrick (November 20, 1859–May 20, 1862)
Ann Patrick (née Wier) (August 24, 1791–1855)
Libby May Humphrey (died 1865, eleven months old)

Lot 45
Phebe Newman (née Smith) (?–1864)

Lot 46
George Tiley (July 14, 1874–1892)
Margaret Tiley (née Story) (?–?)
George Tiley Sr. (?–July 1913)

Lot 47
Multiple unknown burials. Marked as unsold.**

Lot 48
Marked as unsold. Empty.

Lots 49–54
Multiple unknown burials. Marked as unsold.**

Lot 55
Charles Benger (May 23, 1863–November 29, 1933)
Priscilla Benger (née Brooks) (October 18, 1866–December 7, 1940)

Lot 56
Louis Hageman (January 25, 1848–February 14, 1929)
Alberta Hageman (née Hulett) (March 1852–November 2, 1914)**
David Ward Hageman (April 23, 1880–March 9, 1939)
Caroline Hageman (1815–1867)

Lot 57
Chauncey Wheeler (January 3, 1851–January 5, 1929)
Ella Wheeler (née Fulton) (April, 1856–May 26, 1928)
Robert Fulton (March 8, 1854–September 26, 1885)
Joseph Fulton (1772–October 15, 1852)
John Fulton Sr. (1813–1883)
Jane Fulton (née Johnson) (1815–December 10, 1897)

Lot 58
Thomas Moss (February 11, 1811–March 11, 1885)
Isabella Moss (née Crumlich) (c. 1819–March 27, 1848)

Lot 59
Alvah Crandall (July 20, 1804–July 20, 1843) (was not reinterred; remains at BG)

Lot 60
Probably William B. Nobles (1802–1836)

Lot 61
William Frank Mendenhall (May 8, 1889–December 3, 1933)
Elizabeth McCune (?–1872)

Lot 62
Unknown burials. Plat map notations list owner as John Fulton Sr. See lot No. 57.

Lot 63
Unknown burials. Plat map lists Howard Fulton as owner of lot No. 63.

Lot 64
Emanuel Schroeder (January 24, 1850–March 12, 1928)
Anna Schroeder (September 24, 1885–January 28, 1890)
Mary Schroeder (September 24, 1885–February 8, 1890)

Lot 65
James Fullerton (March 6, 1843–November 14, 1929)
Sarah Fullerton (née Chapman) (1841–April 16, 1911)

Lot 66
Plat map lists owner of lot No. 66 as Lester Frundle. Lester is buried in Homewood, Illinois. His mother and brothers are buried in Bachelors Grove Cemetery; see also lot No. 7.

Lot 67
Unknown burials. Plat map lists owner of lot No. 67 as Richard Kropeck, who died in 1985 in Cook County. Burial place unknown at this time.

Lots 68–71
Multiple unknown burials. Marked as unsold.**

Lot 72
Jane Eleanor Fullerton (née Whitehead) (September 14, 1875–April 25, 1925)**

Lot 73
William Rick (March 22, 1871–January 15, 1926)
Mary Rick (née Cague) (October 28, 1875–June 7, 1899)

Lot 74
Charles Hageman (June 4, 1841–March 15, 1924)
Minna Hageman (December 24, 1847–November 10, 1894)

Lot 75
Alvah Orlando Foskett (February 11, 1871–March 9, 1960)
Caroline Sophia Foskett (née Lund) (August 14, 1880–April 29, 1934)

Lot 76
Frederick Earl Gray (died March 22, 1940, seven weeks old)**
Edward F. Gray (March 2, 1935–March 4, 1935)**

Lot 77
John Rick (January 18, 1870–July 9, 1941)
Mary Ellen Rick (née Hopkins) (June 3, 1883–?)**

Lot 78
Theodore Post (1861–Novemer 8, 1924)
Sophie Post (née Flassig) (October 16, 1864–December 31, 1939)

Lot 79
Daniel Newman (April 19, 1871–December 12, 1947)
Dora Newman (née Flassig) (July 25, 1870–October 8, 1948)
Frank Flassig (1828–October 10, 1910)
Dora Flassig (née Mohr) (December 27, 1827–November 16, 1903)

Lot 80
Multiple unknown burials. Plat map notations list owner of lot No. 80 as R. Krueger.

Lot 81
Multiple unknown burials. Plat map notations list owner of lot No. 81 as F. Gray.

Lot 82
Hattie Julie Strutzenburg (née Adams) (February 2, 1909–February 3, 1909)**
Esther Adams (January 19, 1912–July 30, 1913)**
Hattie Therese Adams (née Strutzenberg) (July 13, 1888–December 21, 1913)

Unknown lot numbers hold:

Eliza B. Scott (née Denny) (December 23, 1808–November 1844)
Leonard Scott (1844–1844 or 1845)**
Members of the Stokes family, stones missing after 1935. No burial records found at this time.
Emmeline Dykeman (April 1860–August 5, 1860
Nels Hermansen (?–1869)
Tom Patrick Hanna (1848–1872)
Albion Smith (?–1856)
Thomas Darcy (August 1906–August 1906)

BIBLIOGRAPHY

Newspaper Articles

Blue Island Sun-Standard. "Pioneers in Peaceful Rest: Bachelor's Grove, One of the First Cemeteries; Lies Serene, Undisturbed." August 16, 1935.

Chicago Tribune. "Ex-girlfriend Is Freed in Man's Death." May 7, 1989.

———. "Find Woman Dead Tied Up on Fence." July 19, 1913.

———. "Murder Charges Filed in Hit and Run Death." January 12, 1989.

———. "Murder Suspect Is Found Slain." April 23, 1989.

———. "Mushroom Hunter Finds Woman's Body." September 6, 1966.

———. "7 Seized in Grave Digging." September 14, 1973.

———. "Solution Seen Soon in Cemetery Slaying." May 4, 1989.

———. "Trace Girl Found Dead." September 7, 1966.

———. "Woman on Fence a Suicide." July 20, 1913.

Davis, Richard. "The Bachelor Grove Cemetery Report, circa 1933." *Chicago Now,* October 27, 2012.

Duffin, Mike. "Vandalism Is Most of Attention This Cemetery Gets." *Star,* October 28, 2001.

Fasbinder, Joe. "Ghosts 'Haunt' Cemetery but Vandals Are Its Curse." *Chicago Tribune,* April 18, 1984.

Gamble, Harry. "Is Tiny Cemetery Haunted by Ghosts or Vandals?" *Southtown Economist,* August 24, 1980.

Goering, Laurie. "Man Guilty in Killing of Teen Couple." *Chicago Tribune*, August 19, 1988.

Husar, John. "Satanic Cults Growing in Preserves." *Chicago Tribune*, February 26, 1989.

Karwath, Rob, and Andrew Fegelman. "Suspect Is Charged in Teen Deaths." *Chicago Tribune*, March 4, 1987.

Lee, Amy. "County-run Cemeteries Often Defiled but Not Neglected." *Southtown Star*, July 30, 2009.

Lyson, Elmer. "All Points Southwest." Unknown publication. December 3, 1959.

McNamee, Tom. "Ghostly Past Haunts Cemetery's Shambles—Dead Rest Amid Ruins in South Suburb Graveyard." *Chicago Sun-Times*, October 30, 1992.

Mohr, Michelle. "What's in a Name? Forests and Ponds Bear Witness to Past Luminaries." *Chicago Tribune*, October 23, 1994.

Preston, Mark. "Bachelors Grove: A Non-existent Local Landmark." *Star Tribune*, December 14, 1972.

Reardon, Patrick. "Down Dirt Road: Defacements, Fear and an Eerie Spell." *Suburban Tribune*, July 6, 1977.

Rhodes, Steve. "Does Cook County Neglect Dead People Too?" NBC Chicago local news transcript, July 30, 2009.

Stanley, Charles. "Bachelors Grove Looking for a Little Peace." *Chicago Tribune*, October 30, 2000.

Star Publications. "Do Spirits Roam Bachelors Grove?" October 26, 1986.

Tinley Park Times. "Bachelor Grove Cemetery Discovered by Ripley's Column." August 25, 1933.

Wronski, Richard. "Cemetery Offers Glimpse of Area's First Settlers." *Suburban Economist*, October 27, 1974.

Zorn, Eric. "Satan Worship Called Dangerous, Growing." *Chicago Tribune*, April 27, 1986.

SCIENTIFIC AND ANOMALOUS RESEARCH

The Eddie Schwartz Show (episodes featuring guest Richard T. Crowe) WIND Chicago. 1976–1982.

Houran, James, and Rense Lange. "Predicting Anomalous Effects on Film: An Empirical Test." *Journal of Perceptual and Motor Skills* (1997).

Kaczmarek, Dale. *Bachelors Grove Investigations Throughout the Years.* Ghost Research Society. www.ghostresearch.org.

Persinger, M.A. "The Neuropsychiatry of Paranormal Experiences." *The Journal of Neuropsychiatry and Clinical Neurosciences* 13, no. 4 (2001): 515–24.

———. "Religious and Mystical Experiences as Artifacts of Temporal Lobe Function: A General Hypothesis." 1991.

Persinger, M.A., et al. "The Electromagnetic Induction of Mystical and Altered States Within the Laboratory." *Journal of Consciousness Exploration & Research* 1, no. 7 (2010): 808–30.

Ruttan, L.A., M.A. Persinger and S. Koren. "Enhancement of Temporal Lobe–Related Experiences During Brief Exposures to MilliGauss Intensity Extremely Low Frequency Magnetic Fields." *Journal of Bioelectricity* 9, no. 1 (1990): 33–54.

Supernatural Occurrence Studies Blog.

Time Slips Blog. "The Ultimate Tourist." https://time=slips.blospot.com/2008/03/ultimatetourist.html.

PUBLISHED HISTORICAL RESEARCH

Bettenhausen, Brad L. "Addendum to Batchelors Grove Cemetery and Genealogical Index to the Book Poles of Chicago 1837–1937." *Where the Trails Cross* 27, no. 1. South Suburban Genealogical & Historical Society (Fall 1996).

———. "Batchelors Grove Cemetery." *Where the Trails Cross* 26, no. 1, South Suburban Genealogical and Historical Society (Fall 1995).

Bremen High School Students. *Bremen High School Bicentennial History Project 1976.* Bremen High School, 1976.

Chicago Genealogy Club Newsletter 1, no. 1 (1959).

Plachno, Larry. "The Midlothian and Blue Island Railroad." www.Plachno.com.

Wilkinson, Earnest. "Bachelors Grove Cemetery." *Where the Trails Cross* 7, no. 1, South Suburban Genealogical and Historical Society (Fall 1976).

BOOKS

Andreas, Alfred T. *History of Cook County, Illinois*. Chicago: A.T. Andreas, 1884.

Bielski, Ursula. *Chicago Haunts: Ghostlore of the Windy City*. Chicago: Lake Claremont Press, 1997.

Hanson, George P. *The Trickster & the Paranormal*. N.p.: Xlibris, 2001.

Hucke, Matt, and Ursula Bielski. *Graveyards of Chicago: The People, History, Art & Lore of Cook County Cemeteries*. Chicago: Lake Claremont Press, 1998.

Jarvis, Sharon. *The Uninvited: True Tales of the Unknown*. Vol. 2. New York: Bantam, 1989.

Markus, Scott, and Mary Czerwinski. *Voices from the Chicago Grave*. Holt, MI: Thunder Bay Press, 2008.

Minutes of the Annual Conferences of the Methodist Episcopal Church for the Years 1773–1881. N.p.: Methodist Episcopal Church Conferences, n.d.

Pooley, William Vipond. *The Settlement of Illinois from 1830 to 1850*. Vol. 1. Madison: Bulletin of the University of Wisconsin History Series, 1908.

Schapper, Ferdinand. *Southern Cook County and History of Blue Island Before the Civil War by Ferdinand Schapper of Blue Island, Illinois, and Presented by Him to the Chicago Historical Society, 1917*. Vol. 1. Blue Island, IL: n.d.

Schwartzkopf, Louis J. *The Lutheran Trail*. St. Louis, MO: Concordia Publishing House, 1950.

Scott, Beth, and Michael Norman. *Haunted Heartland*. New York: Stanton & Lee, 1985.

Steiger, Brad. *Psychic City: Chicago, Doorway to Another Dimension*. New York: Doubleday, 1976.

Transactions of the Department of Agriculture of the State of Illinois with Reports from County Agricultural Societies for the Year. Vol. 7. N.p.: Illinois State Journal Company Printers, 1870.

Volp, John Henry. *The First Hundred Years: 1835–1935, an Historical Review of Blue Island, Illinois*. Blue Island, IL: Blue Island Publishing, 1938.

ARCHIVAL MATERIALS

Blue Island Library, clippings files.

Chicago History Museum, map collection.

Cook County Land Records, land ownership records of Bremen Township, Cook County.

Midlothian Library, clippings files.

South Suburban Genealogical & Historical Society, obituary collection.

State of Illinois, land sale records.

Tinley Park Historical Society, various collections.

University of Illinois Archives (Chicago): Forest Preserve District of Cook County Archives, condemnation records of the Forest Preserve District of Cook County.

WEBSITES

Crapia, Pete. Bachelors Grove. www.bachelorsgrove.com.

Illinois Archaeological and Paleontological Resources Protection Act. www.ilga.gov/legislation/ilcs/ilcs3.asp?ActID=375&ChapterID=5.

Illinois Human Skeletal Remains Protection Act. www.ilga.gov/legislation/ilcs/ilcs3.asp?ActID=376.

National Park Service Archaeology Laws and Ethics. www.nps.gov/archeology/public/publicLaw.htm.

The Path to Bachelors Grove. www.thepathtobachelorsgrove.com.

Society for American Archaeology. www.saa.org/ForthePublic/Resources/ArchaeologicalLawEthics/tabid/88/Default.aspx.

Stephenson, John. Bachelors Grove. www.bachelors-grove.com.

About the Author

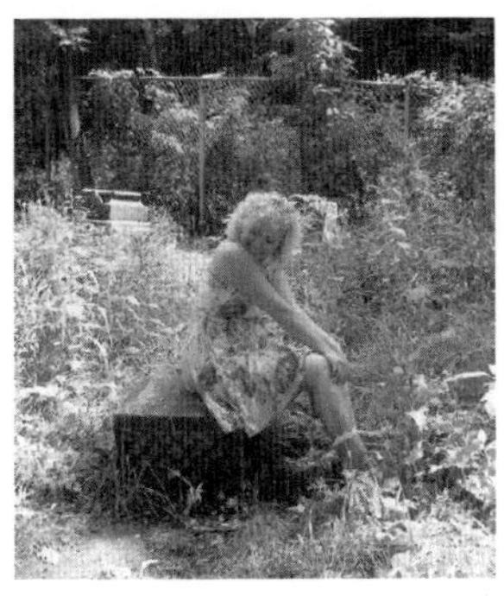

Ursula Bielski is a Chicago historian and folklorist specializing in cemetery history and the folklore of the preternatural. A respected paranormal researcher, she is the author of nine books on Chicago ghost lore and cemetery history and has been studying the settlement, folklore and culture of Bachelors Grove for nearly three decades.

Visit us at
www.historypress.net

This title is also available as an e-book